Beach and Coastal Camping in the Southeast

UNIVERSITY PRESS OF FLORIDA

Florida A&M University, Tallahassee
Florida Atlantic University, Boca Raton
Florida Gulf Coast University, Ft. Myers
Florida International University, Miami
Florida State University, Tallahassee
University of Central Florida, Orlando
University of Florida, Gainesville
University of North Florida, Jacksonville
University of South Florida, Tampa
University of West Florida, Pensacola

Johnny Molloy

University Press of Florida
Gainesville
Tallahassee
Tampa
Boca Raton
Pensacola
Orlando
Miami
Jacksonville
Ft. Myers

Beach *and* Coastal Camping

in the Southeast

11 10 09 08 07 06   6 5 4 3 2 1

A record of cataloging-in-publication data is available from the Library of Congress
ISBN 0-8130-3000-5

Frontis: Grayton Beach State Recreation Area, Florida; *facing page*: Buccaneer
State Park, Mississippi.

The University Press of Florida is the scholarly publishing agency for the State
University System of Florida, comprising Florida A&M University, Florida Atlantic
University, Florida Gulf Coast University, Florida International University, Florida
State University, University of Central Florida, University of Florida, University
of North Florida, University of South Florida, and University of West Florida.

University Press of Florida
15 Northwest 15th Street
Gainesville, FL 32611-2079
http://www.upf.com

This book is for all those who enjoy
sleeping surfside in the Southeast

Other Books by Johnny Molloy

Canoeing & Kayaking Guide to Florida
Canoeing & Kayaking Guide to Kentucky (with Bob Sehlinger)
A Paddler's Guide to Everglades National Park
Beach & Coastal Camping in Florida
A FalconGuide to Mammoth Cave National Park
Land Between the Lakes Outdoor Recreation Handbook
Long Trails of the Southeast
The Best in Tent Camping: The Carolinas
The Best in Tent Camping: Colorado
The Best in Tent Camping: Florida
The Best in Tent Camping: Georgia
The Best in Tent Camping: Kentucky
The Best in Tent Camping: Southern Appalachian & Smoky Mountains
The Best in Tent Camping: Tennessee
The Best in Tent Camping: West Virginia
The Best in Tent Camping: Wisconsin
Day & Overnight Hikes in Shenandoah National Park
Day & Overnight Hikes in the Great Smoky Mountains National Park
Day & Overnight Hikes in West Virginia's Monongahela National Forest
From the Swamp to the Keys: A Paddle through Florida History
Mount Rogers Outdoor Recreation Handbook
The Hiking Trails of Florida's National Forests, Parks, and Preserves
50 Hikes in the North Georgia Mountains
50 Hikes in South Carolina
60 Hikes within 60 Miles: San Antonio & Austin (with Tom Taylor)
60 Hikes within 60 Miles: Nashville
Trial by Trail: Backpacking in the Smoky Mountains

Visit the author's Web site: www.johnnymolloy.com

Contents

Preface

There's something special about camping on the beach—the smell of salt air, the waves lapping you to sleep in your lounge chair, hiking through a maritime forest, kayaking a rich estuary, or taking a long walk astride the sandy surf. When someone yells, "Let's go beach camping!" everyone within earshot wants to come along. But where do you go? Well, if you live in the Southeast or are one of the millions who travel to its coastline every year, then you have a lot of choices.

That's because the Southeast is bordered by ocean from the Texas state line at the Mexican border all the way around the Gulf of Mexico to Key West, then up the Atlantic Coast to Maryland. Some may say Maryland isn't part of the Southeast, but for the greater good of beach campers everywhere, Assateague Island's beautiful seashore is included. This Gulf and Atlantic seashore adds up to thousands of miles of coastline.

Fortunately for beach lovers, a good deal of this beach and coastline has been set aside for public use. A significant portion of this set-aside land is county, state, or national park property, offering a wide array of scenic and rewarding camping experiences: from the world's largest barrier island—Padre Island, Texas—and Gulf Islands National Seashore of Mississippi and Florida to the Florida Keys, the wilderness of Cumberland Island in Georgia, the vast stretches of sand and sea of North Carolina's Outer Banks, and the ponies of Assateague Island National Seashore.

Finding the perfect match between a campground and the needs of your family or group can be difficult, if not overwhelming; campgrounds all have different rules, regulations, and fees. And that's why this guide to beach and coastal camping in the Southeast will come in handy, no matter whether you have a nylon tent, a van, a pop-up camper and pickup truck, or an RV. I have found forty-three of the best places to camp on the beach in the Southeast, and in this book I give you all the details you'll need to decide which of the forty-three is for you. They are all great, and in spite of my best efforts you'll still have trouble deciding!

All forty-three of the campgrounds I discuss here are on public lands. The reason for this is to combine good camping with the natural aspects of America's coastline. Each individual description opens with an overview of the attractions of the campground and what to expect. Then comes a description of what the actual beach and coast are like. Following that is a detailed summary of the features and amenities of the campground. I'll also tell you what times of year are best to visit each place.

A section called Key Information gives explicit directions to the campground and also pertinent data such as Websites, phone numbers, fees, the number of campsites available, regulations, reservation availability, and more. Next for each place is a section called Human and Natural History, which tells a story about the area, perhaps about unusual flora or fauna or sometimes about the effects of human presence on the environment. Sometimes the stories are historical in nature, about an interesting figure or special event connected to a place. Some campgrounds and surrounding areas still show evidence of the native peoples who once lived there.

Then comes a section called What to Do, which gives you some ideas on how to spend your precious free time. I offer suggestions about where to find the best beach walks, historic tours, biking trails, scenic drives, and other natural adventures. If you're into more watery pursuits, you'll appreciate the information on the best swimming, ocean harvesting, snorkeling, canoeing, diving, and pleasure boating you'll find anywhere. Finally, a section called What's Nearby gives you the information you need concerning the indoor and outdoor attractions that lie outside the park boundaries —historic homes, shopping, other and more mainstream tourist attractions.

Now for a word of advice. Before you embark on your camping excursion, learn as much as you can about your destination. If anything in this book is unclear or if you have specific questions about issues not covered here, do call the park before you go there. That way you'll have no unpleasant surprises. If reservations are recommended, by all means make them. Of course, there is a certain appeal to striking out on a whim, and we all do it at times. But being turned away because the campground is full can turn a pleasant outing into fodder for a travel comedy movie. Your limited time will be better spent if you aim to avoid such setbacks.

So set aside some time to read up about where you're going before you pack your gear and strike out on the open road. The beaches and coastlines of the Southeast are waiting for you!

Introduction

The seashore—where land meets water—is a fragile place. Great sand dunes are held in place by sea oats. Living coral reefs grow imperceptibly from the ocean floor. Sea grasses help cleanse the ocean. Estuaries—the breeding grounds for much of the ocean's life—are dependent on just the right mix of salt and fresh water. This delicate balance is constantly in flux. Wind and waves are forever altering the shoreline. Years of island building are wiped out in a single hurricane. The hurricanes of 2004 and 2005 challenged resource managers and closed parks for a time. Sand dunes are moved by the winds. Floods reshape estuarine salt marshes.

And there is one more important agent of change for beach ecosystems—humans. Condos and other developments flatten dunes and channelize marshes. Propellers damage the sea floor. Swimmers and sunbathers dump their trash on the sand and in the water. That's why our shores are more precious now than ever and why it is our responsibility to take care of them. I believe if you go out and see the natural wonders of the southeastern coast, if you build an appreciation for the beauty and diversity of our distinctive natural legacy, you will in turn develop a protective attitude toward the coast and all that it preserves and nurtures.

Humans have long been a presence on our coastlines, and it is truly unrealistic now to expect everyone just to go away. But if we develop the proper attitudes and educate ourselves, we can take those walks on the beach, paddle in the grassy marshes, motor through the salty waters, and snorkel around the reefs while doing minimal damage to the ecosystem. Combining any of those activities with camping is a great way for families and friends to develop an appreciation for our environment and for one another in authentic settings that no theme park can begin to match.

And in the Southeast you will find some of the finest beach camping anywhere. From the dunes and isolation of Padre Island to the tropical and historic Keys, from historic sites around St. Augustine to the lighthouses of the Outer Banks, you'll find lots of similarities but also many subtle differences.

Starting at the Mexican border, nearly all of the Texas coast is lined with barrier islands. The coastline here has wide beaches with some dunes. In many places industry is part of the coastline, for this is where our petrochemical plants and refineries are, processing oil into gasoline and the host of synthetic compounds that drive modern life. Oil rigs are sometimes positioned offshore. That is the way it is. But the birds don't seem to mind, and the Great Texas Coastal Birding Trail extends along the Gulf and includes several of the hottest spots in America for avian enthusiasts.

Louisiana was originally represented in the book by one area, Grand Isle State Park, but that was ground zero for Hurricane Katrina in August 2005; the likely future for the park was unknown as the book went to press, whereas other hurricane-affected camping areas were reopening. The Mississippi coast has sandy beaches and barrier islands but is now also a gambling destination, where casinos have sprung up. Alabama's Gulf State Park is a state jewel.

Florida has more coastline and more campgrounds than any other state in this guidebook. Florida's coast is growing rapidly but the state has actively bought lands to preserve and enjoy. In the Panhandle, barrier islands and peninsulas offer famed sugar-white beaches and gentle waves. The Atlantic side of north Florida is very different. Large waves pound the shore. The vast St. Johns River forms a large estuarine system beyond which lie the Sea Islands, barrier islands that have played host to history and extend northward into Georgia and South Carolina. Central Florida offers both Gulf and Atlantic environments, from the islands of Tampa Bay to the surfing destination of Sebastian Inlet. South Florida has the Everglades and the Keys, which protrude southwesterly into the clear waters of the Gulf and stand as America's most southerly land.

Georgia, one of the original thirteen states, is nothing if not historic. Cumberland Island National Seashore is home to wild horses and mansions, a place where you can see the past and explore a preserved wilderness. Fort McAllister is a place where military history shows up, as it does is a number of the camping destinations in this book. South Carolina offers excellent Atlantic Coast recreation destinations that combine natural fun, history, and developed recreation outside park boundaries, such as at Myrtle Beach State Park. This enables campers to enjoy other coastal pastimes as well as the parks. North Carolina's Outer Banks have a special place in many people's hearts. This strand of sand from Cape Lookout to the Virginia state line is a harsh, changing, and beautiful environment shaped by hurricanes; it has an aura of its own. Campgrounds such as Frisco and Oregon Inlet allow campers to engage with a special slice of these barrier islands.

Farther north, Virginia offers its own share of history at First Landing State Park as well as its share of remoteness on the wild coast of Assateague Island National Seashore. Ocean City, Maryland, has long been a recreational destination for beach lovers. Just south of here lies Assateague State Park and the Old Line State's share of Assateague Island National Seashore.

Beach Hazards

Every year the lure of sand, surf, and sea brings many visitors to the beaches of the Southeast, and the vast majority of beachgoers return home with nothing to ruin the good memories of the trip. There are things to look out for, however. While there's no need to overemphasize negative possibilities, a little self-education can help ensure a positive experience. The warmer times of the year are the most popular beach times. This means hot days—and I do mean hot. Drink plenty of nonalcoholic fluids; keep yourself shaded for a reasonable amount of time, and cool off in the water to prevent symptoms that could lead to heat exhaustion. Most important, the sun alone can do plenty of damage. Occurrence of skin cancer is rising rapidly. By all means wear a hat and use plenty of sunscreen. Of course, shade and clothing are the most effective sunscreens around. I personally try to keep as much of my body covered as I can tolerate.

Beachcombing is a time-honored coastal pastime. Unfortunately, especially in populated areas, trash sometimes washes up on the beach. Watch for glass, nails on boards, and other foot-puncturing items. Consider wearing sandals, especially after the sun starts to go down.

When it's hot, nothing compares with a swim in the ocean. Beaches with lifeguards are ideal, but they are not always an option. Exercise caution when swimming and keep apprised of tide and surf conditions. Showing friends you're strong enough to swim in a rip tide isn't worth the risk. Use an approved flotation device if you feel the slightest bit uncomfortable in the water, and always have someone swimming with you. And, please, always keep an eye on your children when you're near the water. It takes just a moment for a child to be swept out to sea.

You are much more likely to be injured in a car wreck on the way to the beach than to get bitten by a shark, but there are a few oceanic organisms that can ruin your day. Many jellyfish can inflict damage. The most notable is the Portuguese man-of-war, which has tentacles that can cause severe burns and blisters even if the animal is a dead one on the beach. Sea nettles and upside-down jellyfish cause rashes and itching. Not all jellyfish are toxic, but as a rule of thumb, stay away from all jellyfish.

Don't forget that threats run both ways. All of us who want to enjoy America's beautiful coastlines also pose a threat to them. When you interact with coastal environments, tread lightly. Picking sea oats destabilizes the dunes. Driving motorized vehicles in restricted areas tears up the landscape. In your boat, watch your prop and don't motor-dredge in shallow waters. Honor fishing regulations; you know what not to do. Think about what you can do. Be a steward for the land. Together we can make America's coastline the bountiful, beautiful place that we know it can be and should be in the future.

Texas

Isla Blanca County Park
Port Isabel, Texas

If you like being around lots of other beach lovers and also those who live part-time on the beach, Isla Blanca is the place for you. Isla Blanca is the most southerly developed public recreational area in Texas. Being so far south in Texas—at the same latitude as Fort Lauderdale, Florida—this area attracts visitors year-round. Located on South Padre Island, this busy Cameron County park caters during the cooler season to "winter Texans," also known as snowbirds, and to general beach enthusiasts in the spring and summer. Be apprised that despite being a long way from almost everywhere, this slice of the Texas coast may be the most highly developed outside of Galveston.

Figure 1. Fishing the jetty at Isla Blanca.

The park is a veritable city of its own. With more than 700 campsites, Isla Blanca has on the premises a chapel, restaurant, bait shop concession area, marine laboratory—and some prime beachfront. This is a getaway destination where a lot of others will be getting away with you. Some will be there to bask in the warmth, while others will be looking to sample the nightlife of South Padre Island.

The Beach/Coast

Occupying the southern tip of South Padre Island, Isla Blanca sits on some very valuable land; South Padre Island has steadily grown in population and popularity. The Brownsville Ship Channel cuts through the Texas barrier island chain at South Padre, passing just south of Isla Blanca. This makes for some interesting viewing from the shoreline on the south side of the park. A long jetty, often used for fishing by Isla Blanca visitors, extends into the Gulf at the point where the channel meets the open water.

Swinging around to the Gulf side of the park, the beaches begin. The tan sands of the wide beach gently slope into the waves of the sea. A large metal pipe has been placed parallel to the water to keep erosion in check. The first of two sizable park beachfront facilities, the D. J. Lerma Pavilion, is near the southern end of the beach. The pavilion has shaded cabanas, a playground, cold showers, and concessions of all sorts. A day use parking area is nearby. The main beach stretches northward, connected to a large parking area via boardwalk. A second pavilion is at the north end of the park, with many facilities as at the first. Beyond the park stand high-rises and other buildings that crowd the center of South Padre Island. Andy Bowie County Park is at the north end of the island. This park has a birding trail and provides additional beach access, including automobile access; vehicles can drive up the beach on South Padre for several miles.

The Campground

This is easily the largest campground in this guidebook. Like a small city, it has named streets along which the more than 700 campsites are located. The vast majority of the campsites are laid out in a grid, following the street lines. The campground as a whole has a slightly worn look. But in defense of the park, it does have many employees working to keep the facilities intact and running well. The campsites are mostly designed for RVs to be set up side by side without much privacy or space, but they fill just the same. Most RV campsites have water, electricity, and sewer hookups. Winter Texans stay for up to six months at a time during the cooler season. These campers also take advantage of the campsite phone and cable TV services that the park offers. Most of the campground has no view of the ocean, but there are some limited Gulf view sites. A few sporadic palm trees are set among the sites. Bathhouses and trash facilities are spread throughout the camping area. The RV area of the park stays full generally from mid-January through March, and from June through August. Reservations are recommended during these periods.

Tent campers are treated more or less as an afterthought. The designated tent camping areas consist of small sites that are mostly open grassy spots with a stake indicating where the tent should go and with no other facilities. Tent sites are available throughout the year.

Human and Natural History

Padre Island has seen some interesting times and characters. In the early days of European colonization, Europeans plying the Gulf with booty from Mexico attracted pirates, including the infamous Jean Lafitte. Lafitte would often stop on Padre Island to take on fresh water from a well dug near what is now the village of Laguna Vista. Another interesting tale is that of John Singer, brother of the man who invented the Singer sewing machine. John homesteaded on Padre Island after his boat ran aground there in the 1840s. A pro-Union man, Singer left the area when the Civil War heated up, but before departing he buried a fortune in jewelry and coins. After the war the shifting dunes confused him and his wife, and they never found their money. The last battle of the Civil War was in fact fought near here. The Confederates defeated the Union navy, which was trying to block the export of Rebel cotton. Only later did the participants learn that General Lee had surrendered at Appomattox a full month earlier!

What to Do

The beach is the number one draw here. As noted, it is the most southerly developed beachfront in Texas. The pavilion and concession areas serve Isla Blanca patrons, renting umbrellas, chairs, and more for both day users and campers. Surfing and riding "boogie boards" are popular here, especially in the winter months when the surf is up. The jetty that stretches out from the south end of the island is a popular fishing spot and is away from the throngs of sunbathers who congregate here during spring break and in the summer. Park facilities include the bait shop serving the anglers, a bingo hall, and a bicycle and walking trail that circles the campground. The park also has an activity center and an oyster bar. The onsite chapel is nondenominational.

What's Nearby

Just outside the park are all manner of pay-as-you-play beach activities. South Padre Island is an increasingly popular destination that caters to all types of beach enthusiasts, including those who want to enjoy the outdoor offerings of South Texas. Visiting the Dolphin and Nature Research Center is among the wildlife-oriented pastimes here. Windsurfing and kiteboarding are sports of skill practiced on the waters of Laguna Madre, the great estuary protected behind the barrier island. Kite boarding entails riding a small board and being pulled along by a "kite" that is catching the winds. Guided fishing charters are limited only by what you are willing to spend. Other guided tours focus on dolphin watching, snorkeling, and birding. Of course, shopping, dining, and nightlife are to be had in abundance here as well.

Information

Isla Blanca County Park
P.O. Box 2106, Park Road 100
South Padre Island, TX 78597
(956) 761-5494, http://www.co.cameron.tx.us/parks/parks.html
Open: Year-round
Sites: 525 water, electricity, and sewer; 72 water and electricity, 140 tent sites
Amenities: Picnic table
Registration: At park office
Facilities: Hot showers, flush toilets, phone, cable TV
Fees: RV sites $17–$24 per night, depending on amenities; tent sites $12 per night; monthly rates also available
Directions: From Harlingen, Texas, head south on US 77 to Texas 100 (the exit for TX 100 is signposted for South Padre Island). Take Texas 100 east for 27 miles to cross Laguna Madre and reach South Padre Island. Once on the island, take a right at the first light and follow the road, which ends at the park.

Padre Island National Seashore
Corpus Christi, Texas

Padre Island National Seashore is a place of superlatives. For starters, this Texas coastal gem lays claim to being the world's longest barrier island. A staggering 113 miles from end to end, it used to be even longer before the Mansfield Channel, which now marks the island's southern terminus, was cut as a shipping lane in 1964. The national seashore portion of Padre Island extends for 80 miles and ends at Mansfield Channel. And the entire Gulf frontage of the protected national seashore is beach! Here the Gulf crashes into a wide sandy swath flanked by high dunes that reach well back from the coastline. Most of the island remains in a natural state and is accessible only by four-wheel-drive vehicles. However, the park does have some infrastructure in the form of a campground, visitor center, and day use beaches that make it accessible to and enjoyable by all, including those with ordinary passenger cars or a big RV.

The Beach/Coast

At most beach destinations pockets of natural beach are surrounded by civilization. On Padre Island a few pockets of development are surrounded by

Figure 2. Padre Island is the longest barrier island in the world.

nothing but nature, as you will quickly notice upon driving into the national park. The coastal prairie has rolling, vegetation-covered dunes broken by ponds. The crash of the ocean is never far away. Padre Island has so many dunes that one is tempted to call it the Texas Hill Country by the Gulf. From north to south, the first beach access on Padre Island is at North Beach. Then you reach Malequite Beach, which is the main park development and recreation area. Malequite Beach Campground is on the Gulf side of the dunes. Just to the south is the park visitor center, with its ample facilities.

The primary beach access is at the park visitor center, which has a bath-house, shaded picnic area, small grocery, cold showers, informative displays, and an observation deck. Large dunes back the wide beach here, and shaded beachfront picnic cabanas are quickly claimed. A walkway leads to the Gulf. No cars are allowed on this stretch of sand; three miles of beachfront are closed to vehicles.

To the south of Malequite Beach is South Beach, an auto access point where all manner of vehicles drive and camp on the beach for the first four miles. Four-wheel-drive vehicles only are recommended south of the four-mile mark. Intrepid and well-prepared explorers can travel the entire 60 miles of beach reaching southward to Mansfield Channel.

The Campground

Padre Island has many types of camping, from primitive beach camping with no facilities to the organized and designated Malequite Beach Campground. A road breaks through the dunes to reach Malequite Beach. The 42-unit campground is stretched lengthwise along the water with commanding beach and Gulf views. The campsites are situated rather close together. Dunes back the camping area. The sites closest to the beach are the best; sites away from the beach are small and mostly pavement. At each end of the camping area are four tent campsites that have shade cabanas. A beach access trail leads down to the water. Bigger RVs may have trouble pulling into the pull-ins if the campground is crowded. A campground host keeps things safe and organized.

Malequite Beach Campground rarely fills, save during spring break, because there are so many other camping opportunities at Padre Island. Bird Island Basin offers campers a chance to overnight on Laguna Madre, the bay side of Padre Island. Camping is a bit of a free-for-all here with no designated sites, but the area does have some vault toilets. Yarbrough Pass Campground is accessible only by four-wheel-drive vehicle and is also on Laguna Madre.

However, Padre Island is probably best known for its primitive beach camping. A beach access road is located just south of the visitor center. Here visitors can drive right onto the sand, and the first four miles of beach are accessible by all vehicles—yes, you will see RVs driving on the beach! As noted, four-wheel-drive vehicles are needed beyond the four-mile mark, and visitors can camp anywhere along this unbelievably long stretch of wild beach, reaching for 60 miles all the way to Mansfield Channel. Solitude seekers will have no problem here. Free permits, available at the Visitor Center, are required for primitive beach camping.

Human and Natural History

The Karankawa Indians were the first human inhabitants of Padre Island. Their height, propensity to tattoo their faces, and (somewhat erroneous) reputation as cannibals painted them as a fierce tribe to be defeated by European settlers. They were quickly eliminated from the Texas coast through disease and warfare. Spaniards visited the island but left it to nature until Father José Nicolas Balli founded a mission and ranch on the island in the early 1800s. Its early name of White Island (Isla Blanca) faded with time, and the presence of the mission gave rise to the new name of Padre Island. Padre Balli hired help for the ranch and never actually lived there, though his nephew continued operations until the 1850s. The relentless winds, storms, and hurricanes eventually buried the ranch, but the name Padre Island was destined to stick.

What to Do

Padre Island is a natural Gulf experience at its best. The wide, dune-backed beaches are the main draw. Folks can enjoy beachfront with or without their vehicles. Swimming, beachcombing, and surf fishing are the primary activities on the Gulf.

Secondary park activities are birding, windsurfing, and kayaking. The entire park is open to birding, and its many habitats offer changing birding experiences. Up to 350 species of birds visit Padre Island or call it home during the year. Fall and winter are the best times to bird here.

The calmer waters of Bird Basin are popular with those who want to enjoy the recreational opportunities of Laguna Madre. The park's only boat ramp is here. The waters of the bay are usually enjoyed by anglers, who carefully boat the shallows in search of redfish, sea trout, pompano, jack crevalle, and catfish. Surf fishing on the Gulf side yields the same species. Big Shell Beach is purportedly the best surf fishing locale in the park. Both windsurfing and kayaking are popular on Laguna Madre. A seasonal kayak rental facility is located on Laguna Madre at Bird Basin.

Those who want to learn more about the national seashore can enjoy some of the daily interpretive programs, walks, and films about such topics as Gulf turtles, shoreline life, dune formation, and island birds.

What's Nearby

The city of Corpus Christi is within easy striking distance of Padre Island. The town offers a full complement of restaurants and other major city facilities. The Corpus Christi Museum of Science and History is a worthy endeavor. The USS *Lexington*, also known as the "Blue Ghost," is a retired navy battleship that survived the attack on Pearl Harbor on December 7, 1941. You can tour the ship and see artifacts not only from this ship but also from the USS *Arizona*, which was sunk during the day that would "live in infamy," as FDR put it. Visit the Texas State Aquarium, which features freshwater and saltwater life that you as a beach camper will surely enjoy.

Information

Padre Island National Seashore
P.O. Box 181300
Corpus Christi, TX 78480
(361) 949-8068, www.nps.gov/pais
Open: Year-round
Sites: 34 pull-in sites, 8 tent sites, unlimited completely primitive beach and bay camping
Amenities: Picnic table; some sites have shade cabanas
Registration: Self-registration onsite
Facilities: Cold showers, flush toilets, water spigots
Fees: $8 per night at Malequite Beach, $5 per night at Bird Basin, primitive camping free
Directions: From Corpus Christi, take TX 358 east until it becomes Park Road 22. Follow Park Road 22 across Laguna Madre onto Padre Island and continue south to enter the park.

Mustang Island State Park
Corpus Christi, Texas

The long, low spit of grass, water, dune, and sand known as Mustang Island State Park preserves a natural slice of the Texas coast. A wide beach and more than five miles of Gulf frontage add up to a lot of sandy shoreline to explore. Some of the highest dunes in Texas are found here, behind these wide beaches. Campers have two options—one can rough it directly on the Gulf with primitive tent camping or enjoy the amenities of a fully equipped RV camping area on the coastal prairie away from the beach. Beachcombing, relaxing, fishing, and surfing are some of the most common pastimes at this safe, family-oriented state park.

The Beach/Coast

Mustang Island is a north-south-oriented barrier island that protects the wide mouth of Corpus Christi Bay. As with other barrier islands connected to land by bridges, it faces growth pressure. However, the State of Texas protects and manages a 4,000-acre swath of this island facing the Gulf. This setup

Figure 3. Mustang Island State Park has a wide beach.

allows for miles of natural Lone Star beach, plenty of room for the crabs, a few beach chairs, a few cars, and people out escaping the rigors of daily life. At the center of the park is a bathhouse on pilings, which offers a view into the Gulf, along the impressive dune line, and into the coastal prairie away from the beach. Below this is the primary day use area, where cars are not allowed on the beach. A series of picnic tables shaded by cabanas stand parallel to the wide, imperceptibly sloping beach. Heading north along the beach takes you to the area favored by anglers and surfers. A pair of jetties extends into the Gulf, channeling Water Exchange Pass. The park beach camping area extends south of the beachfront bathhouse. This is the longest stretch of park beach. Water spigots, cold showers, and trash cans back against the dunes. The quieter waters of Corpus Christi Bay gently wash against the bay shore of Mustang Island.

The Campground

The RV camping area is a mixed bag. It is set about a quarter mile back from the beach amid grassy coastal prairie. It has 48 campsites, each with full hookups, including 50-amp, 30-amp, and 110-volt electrical outlets. Water is at each site, as are an upright grill and a picnic table shade by a wooden cabana. Unfortunately, the State of Texas used a lot of pavement here, giving the place a parking lot aspect and cutting down its aesthetic appeal. Nary a tree is to be found, which is at least consistent with the coastal prairie environment, if short on visual interest. Since no one gets an ocean view, all sites are equal; those closest to the bathhouse seem to fill first. The bathhouse is fully equipped with hot showers and flush toilets. The other camping option is directly on the Gulf of Mexico. Campers drive directly onto the beach and head south down the sand to choose a spot. Several shady picnic tables are strung along the beach against the dunes, and these sites are the first to go. Solitude can be had by going farther down the beach, except at busy times. Water spigots are strategically situated beside the dunes and portable toilets are set out according to camping demand.

The RV campground fills every day from January through late March, then things slack off. It fills daily again from June through August. Reservations are highly recommended during these times. The beach camping area is never completely filled, and those who want to overnight here are never turned away. Potential beach campers should call ahead to find out if the beach is drivable. It usually is, but it can sometimes get powdery after excessively dry periods.

Human and Natural History

The dunes of Mustang Island are important to the overall ecosystem of this barrier island. Winds blowing off the Gulf of Mexico build up these dunes, with a little help from such plants as sea oats and morning glory. The plants and their roots form an infrastructure upon which the dunes can rise. The highest dunes are often the most vegetated. Dunes can reach up to 35 feet on Mustang Island but average approximately 20 feet. Barrier islands and their dunes are not only attractive but functional as well: they absorb impact from hurricanes, providing the first defense for bays and the mainland.

What to Do

In southeast Texas people can find many public beach access points, but some of them can be rough and turn into party spots, especially after the sun goes down. Mustang Island State Park, on the other hand, provides a protected and patrolled destination that minimizes such concerns. It is on the quiet side, and rangers see to it that the park remains a family-oriented destination. Park users enjoy all manner of beach activities—shelling, surf fishing, surfing, windsurfing, and what one ranger called "family frolicking": when families play in the surf and enjoy that special parcel of earth where the land meets the sea. Sometimes parents hang out under an umbrella with a book and watch their offspring do the frolicking. Visitors have the choice of being in the area without cars or having the car at hand for easy access to gear and supplies. Besides providing beach recreation, this state park is here to preserve the resource, and rangers hold interpretive programs on weekends and some evenings, helping visitors learn about the park's birds, geography, history, wildlife, and shoreline ecology.

What's Nearby

Have you ever wanted to ride a horse along the beach like you've seen in the movies? Here is your chance. Mustang Riding Stables is located north of the park; their phone number is (361) 749-5055. You can head down the beach riding your own mustang. To the north, Port Aransas is a coastal town without the overdeveloped atmosphere of other island towns.

Or you can visit the Texas State Aquarium in Corpus Christi to see the dolphins, sharks, and other aquatic life inhabiting the Gulf of Mexico. For a distinctively Texas touch, the aquarium features a re-created oil rig where visitors can see the kinds of marine life forms that gather around these submerged structures offshore.

Information

Mustang Island State Park
P.O. Box 326
Port Aransas, TX 78373
(361) 749-5246, www.tpwd.state.tx.us; camping reservations (512) 389-8900
Open: Year-round
Sites: 48 RV sites, unlimited beach camping sites
Amenities: RV sites have electricity, water, shaded picnic table, upright grill; some beach campsites have shaded picnic tables
Registration: At park headquarters building
Facilities: Hot showers, flush toilets, pay phone
Fees: RV sites $15 per night; primitive beach campsites $7 per night
Directions: From Corpus Christi, take TX 358 east until it becomes Park Road 22. Continue on Park Road 22 to TX 361. Turn left on TX 361 and follow it 5 miles to the park, on your right.

Goose Island State Park

Rockport, Texas

Sometimes, when going beach camping, I get sun-whipped and wish for some shade. At Goose Island State Park the beautiful oak woods back from the water allow for such shady luxury. But campers also have the option of setting up out in the sun with a gorgeous view of Aransas Bay. This bayside state park just north of Corpus Christi offers recreational options as well as camping options. Anglers of all stripes come here, from hardcore fishermen taking out their own boats to folks who enjoy all the fishing piers on this section of the coast; those who want to hire fishing guides will find plenty in the greater Corpus Christi area. A bona fide beach is not far from the park, as are other attractions outside Goose Island. The large Aransas National Wildlife Refuge nearby is a part of the Gulf coast that is a big-time birding destination. Goose Island was the first designated birding spot on the Texas Coastal Birding Trail.

The Beach/Coast

Set on the Lamar Peninsula, which juts into the large Aransas Bay, the park consists of a swath of coastal land and Goose Island, which is connected to the mainland by a small bridge. Smaller St. Charles Bay and Copano Bay

Figure 4. Waterfront camping at Goose Island State Park.

border the Lamar Peninsula. The mainland area of the park is characterized by beautiful live oak woodland broken by alluring meadows. Goose Island itself is a long narrow spit of land that is mostly shells and grass and is backed by a wetland. The views from Goose Island are extensive, reaching as far as the eye can see into the bay. A long fishing pier owned by the state park extends seaward from the east end of Goose Island. A seawall borders the bay side of the island. Beyond this seawall is a shallow tidal area with many oyster bars to be seen when the tides expose them. Occasional steps lead down to the shallows, though the shallows are not conducive to swimming and swimming here is not recommended. There are better swimming destinations nearby. Matagorda Island lies across Aransas Bay, between the park and the Gulf, which means the bay waters are well protected.

The Campground

Water lovers will flock to the bayfront camping area. After crossing the bridge to Goose Island, the access road splits. To the left is Trout Street, with campsites #1–#24. Fifteen waterfront campsites overlook the water from atop a seawall with direct and wide open views of Aransas Bay. This setup keeps the breezes blowing and the shade minimal. Each campsite has electricity, water, a standup grill, and a covered picnic table. Campers pull their rigs broadside to the Gulf and enjoy the scenery. The sites are big enough for any RV.

The other ten sites are on the "back" side of the island and are less popular. Redfish Road has campsites #25–#44. The only differences between these and the Trout Street campsites is that these have less room between the seawall and the picnic shelter, and all sites are waterfront. The rest of the campground, the woodland part, is landward, amid lovely and picturesque oaks. The landward campsites are mostly shaded, are well spaced apart, and have ample vegetation between them for privacy. These are among the prettiest coastal campsites in Texas. Budget-minded campers can go for some of the walk-in and drive-up tent sites that don't have electricity. Four fully equipped bathhouses serve the whole campground. Usage patterns depend on the season. In winter the woodland sites are most popular. In summer the bayfront sites are the first to go. The bayfront sites fill just about every weekend in the summer. The woodland sites go next, and the walk-in tent sites are the last to fill.

Human and Natural History

One of Texas' most prized possessions is on these state park grounds: the tree simply known as the Big Tree. Located just a little farther inland than the oaks under which we can overnight is the State Champion Live Oak, protected within Goose Island State Park. Its trunk is more than 35 feet in circumference! Its crown spreads nearly 90 feet in width, despite the tree being only 44 feet high. You must see this giant; it is believed to be 2,000 years old. Since its value has been recognized, it has received a little help late in life in the form of branch trimming, crack patching, and pest control. The Big Tree is just a short drive from the camping area of the state park.

What to Do

Fishing and lying about fishing are the main pastimes at Goose Island. Actually, the fishing is good enough in greater Aransas Bay to avoid any need for tall tales. As mentioned, the park has its own fishing pier, and many anglers choose to fish from the seawall by the bayfront campsites. A boat launch at the park makes it easy to motor for redfish, flounder, mangrove snapper, and trout. A bait shop operates near the boat launch on warm weekends. A fish-cleaning station aids in turning your catch into dinner. If you prefer to be guided to the fish of your choice, there are plenty of able fellows around to lead the way. Check with the park office or the Rockport-Fulton Area Chamber of Commerce for a list of guides. Self starters can also go to the nearby Copano Bay State Fishing Pier for more fishing opportunities. Beach lovers won't be left out, as Rockport Beach Park is a first-rate sandy shoreline complete with facilities such as covered picnic shelters, a fishing pier of its own, and a bird sanctuary. The state park and this park are just two of many destinations on the Great Texas Coastal Birding Trail.

What's Nearby

The 57,000-acre Aransas National Wildlife Refuge borders Goose Island State Park and effectively increases the protected area acreage manifold. The refuge offers many chances to interact with the wild world. A 16-mile loop road provides access to the refuge. It protects the complex intertwined world of land and water—fresh water and salt water. Whooping cranes are the refuge's chief claim to fame in the birding world, but there are also plenty of other birds and land animals to see. Stop at the wildlife interpretive center before trying some of the seven or so miles of trails, or check out the view from on high at the observation tower.

Information

Goose Island State Park
202 South Palmetto Street
Rockport, TX 78382
(361) 729-2858, www.tpwd.state.tx.us; camping reservations (512) 389-8900
Open: Year-round
Sites: 44 bayfront sites, 56 fully equipped woodland sites, 25 water-only tent sites
Amenities: Bayfront sites have electricity, water, upright grill, covered picnic shelter; fully equipped woodland sites have the same as bayfront sites plus fire ring and lantern post; woodland tent sites do not have electricity
Registration: At park entrance booth
Facilities: Hot showers, flush toilets, pay phone
Fees: Bayfront sites $16 per night; fully equipped woodland sites $14 per night, tent sites $9 per night
Directions: From Rockport, take TX 35 north for 10 miles to Park Road 13. Turn right on Park Road 13 and follow it 2 miles to the park, on your right.

Quintana Beach County Park

Freeport, Texas

Situated at the mouth of the Brazos River, Quintana Beach is rich in history in addition to being a pleasant place to camp and enjoy a section of the Gulf of Mexico. The beachfront is not overly long but will suffice for most users. In addition to Quintana Beach, Brazoria County has more than 23 miles of other beaches to enjoy. With a mix of RV sites, primitive tent camping sites, and even cabins on a beachfront hill, your overnighting concerns are well addressed here. One of the early visitors who stayed a while was none other than Texas legend Stephen Austin, who founded the hamlet of Quintana back in 1824. The town never really grew, but some historic homes have been preserved on the park grounds. These add a historic touch to the park, and much of its infrastructure has been built with a rustic theme to enhance the pioneer air supplied by the old homes.

The Beach/Coast

The Brazos River runs just north of Quintana Beach. With the establishment of the Gulf Intracoastal Waterway and the expansion of the Brazos to make a major waterway entering the nearby town of Freeport, extensive jetties were

Figure 5. Winter brings big waves and debris into Quintana.

built seaward from the mouth of the Brazos. A sandy beach extends along the park shore from the south jetty. Above the jetty is a manmade hill that was once part of fortifications for elevated gun turrets dating from World War II. This hill offers good vistas of the beach below and the mouth of the river in the distance. A gun turret and cabins now stand atop the hill.

Heading southward along the beach you will notice the plethora of driftwood that gathers here. Whole tree trunks churn down the Brazos River during times of flood. They are washed out into the Gulf and then pushed back to the shoreline by continuous wave action. The driftwood gives the beach character and is an enhancement in my opinion. A lighted fishing pier is at the far south end of the park, extending toward the Gulf. However, as a practical matter, more fishermen gather along the rock jetty extending far into the sea beside the Brazos than gather at the fishing pier. Shaded shelters, picnic tables, and outdoor showers are located just behind the surprisingly high dunes at the park beach.

The Campground

The campground at Quintana Beach offers overnighting options for both RVers and tent campers. Big rigs can camp in either Spoonbill Circle or Heron Court, a good 200 yards inland from the beach. Heron Court, with 20 campsites, is laid out in two loops and has back-in sites that are laid out like the spokes of a wheel. Grass surrounds the concrete pads and a few palm trees provide minimal shade. Spoonbill Circle, with 32 sites, is laid out in two ovals. Premium pull-through sites offering 50-amp service are on the interior of the area, which is also surrounded by grass punctuated with a few palms. The sites on the outside of the ovals are the back-in variety. All the RV sites have water, electricity, a standup grill, and a picnic table. The third camping area is the primitive tent area. This is in a grassy field behind the elevated gun turret mound. Campers have to park and walk a distance to the sites. Scattered picnic tables are the only amenities at these sites. A second, smaller tent camping area is closer to the beach near the group fire ring. Breezes are better here, but you are located very near the park cabins and shelters. Both RV and tent campers are served by a bathhouse that has hot showers, flush toilets, and a laundry. Plans are in the works to expand the campground with more RV sites. Electric and water hookups have been laid to this effect. Open year-round, the campground fills from June through August. Reservations are recommended during this time. Primitive tent campers can nearly always get a campsite.

Human and Natural History

Located on the south side of the mouth of the Brazos River, Quintana County Park has seen much history. After Stephen F. Austin laid out the town, it became a modest trade and shipping center. Union gunboats sought to interrupt trade during the Civil War, and the Confederates built Fort Velasco across the river from the current park. The fort saw little action. The town grew slowly until the Hurricane of 1900, when the settlement was nearly demolished and commerce was halted. Later a waterway was cut connecting the Brazos to Galveston Island, but this and other improvements mostly benefited the upstream town of Freeport. Industrial development has since characterized the nearby inland areas, while Quintana has remained quaint. The establishment of the county park and the protection of the homes inside it enhanced the village.

What to Do

This county park is a quiet destination that is a little harder to reach than other places. And without a nearby town like Galveston for action seekers, it remains a peaceful getaway for those who favor the quiet. Beachcombers can search for shells; the peak shelling season is in winter, December through February. Searching for appealing pieces of driftwood is productive here, and the abundance of driftwood also leads to more nighttime beach fires. Anglers can fish on the lighted park pier, from the jetty along the Brazos, or in the surf. Common catches are redfish, speckled trout, and flounder. The town of Quintana has established a small park of its own: the Neotropical Bird Sanctuary just across from the town hall has trails that wind among the woods and past ponds. Other nearby birding destinations are San Luis Pass to the north and Brazos Bend State Park. The county park has an enclosed play area for kids and has numerous group shelters. It also features a volleyball net and horseshoes for those so inclined. Overall, Quintana exudes a slow, small-town feel that attracts those who want to relax.

What's Nearby

San Bernard National Wildlife Refuge is located south of Quintana. Marshes, bottomlands, tidelands, lightly forested areas, and ponds are great for birding, fishing, photography, and hiking. Take your vehicle on Cocklebur Slough Road and beside Moccasin Pond. You can observe avian life in varied settings. Get out of your car and take the Bobcat Woods Trail in Cocklebur

Slough. A boardwalk leads to a watery overlook. The Cow Trap Trail traverses marshland and open prairie pocked with small ponds. Look for ibis and other wading birds here. Paddlers can quietly stroke their blades in the Cedar Lakes area.

Information

Quintana Beach County Park
330 5th Street
Quintana, TX 77541
(800) 872-7578, www.quintana-tx.org
Open: Year-round
Sites: 56 RV sites, 27 primitive tent sites
Amenities: RV sites have water, electricity, standup grill, picnic table
Registration: At park office
Facilities: Hot showers, flush toilets, laundry, pay phone
Fees: Pull-through RV sites $20 per night May–September, $18 per night rest of year; back-in RV sites $18 per night May–September, $17 per night rest of year; tent sites $15 per night May–September, $12 per night rest of year
Directions: From near Brazoria, take TX 36 south to FM 523. Turn right on FM 523 and follow it for 1 mile, then veer left onto FM 1495. Stay with FM 1495 for 4 miles to Brazoria County Road 723. Turn left on CR 723 and follow it for 2.2 miles to a T-junction. Turn right at the T-junction and enter the park.

Galveston Island State Park
Galveston, Texas

This state park offers a quality camping destination on a Texas barrier island near Houston. Covering 2,000 acres of Gulf front and bay lands, it is not only the beach but the entire protected ecosystem that makes this state park special. Its Gulf shoreline nearly two miles long attracts beach lovers, and the rest of the park will keep you returning for more. Outdoor activities include fishing, birding, kayaking, hiking, and beachcombing. Camping opportunities are varied, including duneside camping in the Gulf breezes and bayside camping for those who want to be on the quieter side of the island. Enclosed camping shelters provide overnighting venues for rainy or buggy times. The city of Galveston is nearby—but not too close—if you want to indulge in citified beach fun in addition to the natural alternatives at the state park.

Figure 6. Sea oats and a wooden fence protect the shore at Galveston Island State Park.

The Beach/Coast

Luckily for us, the protected segment of this park encompasses a portion of Galveston Island from the waters of West Bay all the way across to the waters of the Gulf of Mexico. This way we can enjoy the varied landscape of this island. The two miles of park beaches are backed by dunes with erosion fences on them to keep the dunes intact and to channel human traffic over wooden walkways. The beaches of the city of Galveston are raked of seaweed and natural debris, but the beaches here are left in their natural state, for beach debris actually helps stabilize the sand and keeps the beach here for future visitors. Shelling can be good at the state park, especially in the winter.

Freshwater marshes and ponds are scattered inland. The bay side of the island is made up of a series of estuarine inlets and grassy flats that form an important facet of the barrier island coastal ecosystem. These tidal wetlands provide key nursery areas for many forms of marine life. Visitors can access the wetlands by kayak and can also view them via trails leading to elevated platforms. These marshlands are an important bird habitat.

The Campground

Galveston Island State Park has three types of camping opportunities. The primary camping area has 150 sites in a series of three loops located on the Gulf just behind the dune line. The rolling surf is clearly audible and visible from your rig at the beachfront campsites. Each of these sites has water, electricity, an upright grill, and a sheltered picnic table. The sites have paved pull-ins surrounded by grass. There is no other vegetation between sites, meaning little campsite privacy. However, this setup keeps the breezes flowing and the views good. Campground #1, with sites #1–#50, has 50-amp hookups, while the Campgrounds #2 and #3 have 30-amp hookups. Each of the three camping area has its own bathhouse.

The two other camping areas are near the bay side of the island. The 10 camping shelters are located in a loop of their own with a bathhouse in the center. These shelters are in high demand when the rains come or when the bugs are biting, which is usually after prolonged rains. Shelters are roofed, with a door and screen windows. The last camping area is the group trailer section. This is set along the edge of dry land overlooking extensive grass beds and the waters of West Bay. Each campsite has a paved pull-in, water, and electricity but no picnic table. However, a shaded shelter with picnic tables is located in the center of the circle. This camp is the quietest in the park.

The busy season here lasts from March through November, during which period the park is nearly always full at weekends. Be apprised that the campground can also fill on any day of the week from June through August. Reservations are highly recommended during high summer. Sites at Campgrounds #1–#3 and the camping shelters can be reserved. The group trailer area is first come, first served only.

Human and Natural History

This beachfront is not only pretty but also historic. Members of the ill-fated Narváez Spanish expedition were wrecked here in 1528 after leaving Florida when their supply ships never arrived there. From this point forty men of the expedition continued a difficult and deadly journey south along the Gulf of Mexico and to inland Mexico—then New Spain. They might have had a different opinion about camping on Galveston Island than we do today. Ultimately only four men arrived in what is now Mexico City, after eight harrowing years.

What to Do

This state park is good for beachcombing. Shells were certainly present in abundance during my winter stay. The beach is the main attraction here, despite there being many miles of public beaches on the populated busy east side of Galveston Island. Generally people who come to the park for shelling head for the sandy swath where the land meets the salt water.

Active visitors can look beyond the beach. On the bay side of the park there are more than five miles of trails open for hiking and biking. These trails, collectively known as the Clapper Rail Trail, explore the wetlands and bayous where the land meets West Bay. Boardwalks, wildlife viewing spots, and elevated overlooks enhance the experience. Birding is big here. You can learn more about this complex ecosystem at the park nature center. In summer an interpretive ranger leads beach walks, bay walks, and bird walks.

Some fishermen use the trails to access the West Bay tidal shallows, also seeking bass in freshwater ponds. You may even see an alligator in the ponds. Others go kayaking in the bays and inlets. The park has established a kayaking launch on Oak Bayou. But most anglers are going for saltwater fare, such as reds, trout, and flounder. Surf fishing on the Gulf side is popular too.

What's Nearby

The city of Galveston is a short drive east from the park. This beach town has all the variety expected of such a town, from seafood buffets to bars and souvenir shops. Galveston specializes in themed tourist events, such as Mardi Gras, motorcycle rallies, art shows, boat parades, fishing tournaments, and more. Many visitors camp at the park and head into town to enjoy the best of both worlds.

Information

Galveston Island State Park
14901 FM 3005
Galveston Island, TX 77554
(409) 737-1222, www.tpwd.state.tx.us; camping reservations (512) 389-8900
Open: Year-round
Sites: 170 sites with water and electricity; 10 camping shelters
Amenities: Water, electricity; most sites have covered picnic tables
Registration: At park headquarters
Facilities: Hot showers, flush toilets, pay phone
Fees: Beachfront campsites $20 per night; others $15 per night; camping shelters $20 per night
Directions: From exit 1 on I-45, take 61st Street south to Seawall Boulevard. Turn right on Seawall Blvd., which is FM 3005, and follow it 10 miles to the park.

Sea Rim State Park

Port Arthur, Texas

Sea Rim State Park is known as much for its birding as for its beaches. This sandy swath of southeast Texas is famed as a stopover spot for migratory songbirds crossing the Gulf of Mexico. It is primarily the canebrakes, shrubs, and occasional trees that attract the passing songbirds—not the shoreline. Extensive wetlands on this 15,000-acre tract also provide a haven for waterfowl. Besides the migrants, many birds call Sea Rim State Park home year-round, and the number and variety of birds to be seen here lure an ever-increasing number and variety of birders to the park. But don't discount the beaches at Sea Rim; the beaches draw in people who want to relax along the Gulf Coast and enjoy the natural atmosphere of the area—and the beaches also draw in shorebirds that birders enjoy. Three types of camping experiences can be had here, from RV camping with water and electricity or tent camping with amenities to completely primitive beach camping.

Figure 7. The surf leaves an interesting pattern at Sea Rim.

The Beach/Coast

Sea Rim State Park protects five miles of coastline, of which three miles are pure beach. The other two miles are mud flats. What visitors need to know is that, large as Sea Rim State Park is, it is bordered on both sides by federal wildlife refuges, which of course greatly increase the scale of the protected landscape and provide a natural and quiet atmosphere over a large area. Furthermore, even beyond the conserved lands, this part of the Texas coast is little populated and really lends a feeling of being "out there." As a result, supply runs can be long, so stock up before you go out to Sea Rim.

Bordering the park's beach on one side is the East Beach Primitive Camping Area, where campers can pull cars directly onto the sand and camp. Head west, and the next section is the day use beach area, where the sand slowly rises toward surprisingly low dunes. Autos are not allowed on the beach here. Picnic tables are strung along the back of the beach line in places. Walkways connect the beach to parking areas. The main visitor center is near the day use beach, and it has shaded picnic tables and an observation deck that allows you to look over your sand and sea empire. Farther west, the West Beach Primitive Camping Area begins. This camping beach is longer than the eastern camping area.

The Campground

Although the primitive beach camping is fine, the two developed camping areas at Sea Rim State Park are the weak link of your overall experience here. The RV camping area is next to the main visitor center, just across low dunes from the beach. On first inspection you may think you are simply looking at a parking lot; upon closer inspection, you will realize the RV camping area is indeed a parking lot. It has 20 sites that are all on pavement and have water and electricity hookups and a picnic table at the edge of the pavement. Ten of the campsites are beachside. The second developed camping area is for tents. It has 10 campsites. The sites are in an open grassy locale just behind the low dunes. Spanish bayonet and cane border parts of the camping area. Elevated tent pads keep campers dry at night. However, the sites on the marsh side of the road are low, and the elevated tent pads may be the only dry areas left after a big thunderstorm.

At the two primitive beach camping areas the only amenities are garbage cans. As indicated, the West Beach Primitive Camping Area is the more popular than the East, being longer and wider.

A full bathhouse with hot showers is located at the park headquarters building. Sea Rim State Park is busy from late April through August. Birders fill the campgrounds in spring, and then families keep it busy through the summer. Alcohol is not allowed at the park, which keeps college kids and partiers away. Reservations are recommended during summer months, even though primitive beach campers are never turned away.

Human and Natural History

Sea Rim State Park is bordered by McFaddin National Wildlife Refuge on one side and Texas Point National Wildlife Refuge on the other. Together the three amount to 75,000 acres of important feeding and resting areas for migrating and wintering populations of waterfowl. The two refuges contain large freshwater marshes as well as brackish marsh and salt marsh. Occasional slightly higher ground harbors wooded uplands and prairie ridges.

Wildlife is abundant in these areas as well as Sea Rim. Geese and ducks congregate in large numbers during the cooler times of year. As spring comes along migrating songbirds fly through the upper Texas coastal region, with peak migration occurring in April. They are returning from winter in Central and South America. Warblers, vireos, grosbeaks, tanagers, orioles, and buntings are but a few of the nearly 280 species of birds found on both refuges.

What to Do

Beach visitors like to swim in the Gulf. Others enjoy the beach chairs and umbrellas that the park rents out during the warm months. Beach lovers may also be surf fishing. In the fall, surf fishermen will be angling for redfish. Other catches are sea trout, flounder, and black drum. Wintertime is the best time for beachcombing and gathering shells.

Birders are to be seen all over the park, but a special draw is the Gambusia Nature Trail. This is a three-quarter-mile boardwalk over marsh terrain where many birds are found. The Willow Pond Birding Trail is a good choice for those wanting to add to their birding "life list," especially during the springtime migration of neotropical songbirds. People also like to spot alligators here. Jefferson County, where Sea Rim State Park is located, has the highest concentration of alligators in the state of Texas.

The marsh unit, across TX 87, also provides birding opportunities. Birders can go out by boat, as there is a boat ramp, and the park provides canoes and paddleboats for rent. There are wildlife observation decks and even wooden camping platforms for those who want to overnight in the marsh. During the warm season, visitors can explore the marsh in a different way—on an airboat tour. Try one if you have never done it.

What's Nearby

Sabine Pass State Park and Historic Site is located near Sea Rim State Park. During the Civil War Union and Confederate forces tangled here at the mouth of the Sabine River. The Sabine was important to the Rebels, as shipments of gunpowder and supplies passed through. Fort Sabine was initially occupied by the South but abandoned. The Confederates later erected another fort upstream on the Sabine, which was attacked by the Yankees. This time, with the improved fort and with accurate cannon fire, the Davis Guard turned back the Union forces, keeping Texas in the hands of the South. The Davis Guard was the only group honored by the Confederate Congress during the Civil War. Today you can visit Sabine Pass and enjoy the interpretive information along with the attractive natural setting, which also offers fishing, hiking, and camping.

Information

Sea Rim State Park
19335 Highway 87
P.O. Box 1066
Sabine Pass, TX 77655
(409) 971-2559, www.tpwd.state.tx.us; camping reservations (512) 389-8900
Open: Year-round
Sites: 20 RV sites, 10 developed tent sites, unlimited primitive beach sites
Amenities: RV sites have picnic table, electricity, and water; developed tent sites have tent pad, upright grill, and fire ring
Registration: At park entrance booth
Facilities: Hot showers, cold showers, flush toilets, pay phone
Fees: RV sites $12 per night; developed tent sites $9 per night; primitive beach tent sites $7 per night
Directions: From exit 873 on I-10, just west of the Louisiana border, take TX 73 west/TX 62 south for 4.5 miles onto TX 87 south. Turn right on TX 87 south and follow it through the town of Port Arthur and onward for a total of 41 miles to reach the state park on your left.

Mississippi

Davis Bayou, Gulf Islands National Seashore
Ocean Springs, Mississippi

When driving into Davis Bayou, you enter a shady haven of natural coastal woodland a few miles east of Biloxi. Davis Bayou is part of the Mississippi Unit of Gulf Islands National Seashore. Separated by the state of Alabama from the Florida Unit of the national seashore, Davis Bayou includes an auto-accessible mainland section, where you can camp among live oaks, take in the coastal forest, hike, fish, and enjoy the visitor center. Five protected islands lie offshore and offer excellent exploring opportunities, but only one can be reached by public passenger ferry: West Ship Island. Remote as some barrier islands are, the local towns are readily accessible from the mainland portion of the national seashore. This makes visiting the casinos and other attractions of greater Biloxi easy, yet you can return to your protected world of Davis Bayou.

Figure 8. Davis Bayou has a rich estuarine environment.

The Beach/Coast

Davis Bayou itself is a coastal estuarine tidal basin. This basin is surrounded by spartina grass and opens to the Gulf. A portion of the park borders Davis Bayou and overlooks the estuary. Most of the park borders some smaller tidal creeks that feed into Davis Bayou. The park fishing ramp leads into Halstead Bayou, while much of the park borders Stark Bayou. The visitor center overlooks yet another tidal creek. To enjoy the coastal sands, beach enthusiasts need to leave the park and return to US 90 and Biloxi, which advertises 26 miles of beaches. The coast at Biloxi was being becoming built up with casinos and other tourist attractions when Hurricane Katrina swept in and changed everything. Public beaches are located along the shoreline amid the rebuilding.

Those with self-propelled craft—kayaks and canoes—can set out from the park boat ramp and paddle out to Deer Island, which is about a 45-minute paddle. Deer Island is managed by the State of Mississippi and has a beach. The other Mississippi Gulf islands are part of the national seashore and are accessible by private boat. Petit Bois Island is the farthest east, near Alabama. Horn Island is a scenic destination but is a challenging trip with a kayak. East Ship Island comes next. West Ship Island is served by a passenger ferry and is thus the most popular. The island has a lighthouse, historic Fort Massachusetts, a fine swimming beach overlooking the Gulf, and beachcombing opportunities for all. Cat Island is the most westerly of the islands, but parts of it are privately owned.

The Campground

The campground at Davis Bayou has many ideal characteristics and makes for a quality coastal camping destination. It is a quiet, wooded, and peaceful retreat in the fast-growing greater Biloxi area. The grounds are well maintained and naturally appealing. A key asset is that with only 52 sites, this campground is the right size for a sense of retreat. Campsites are large and adequately spaced from one another, and all of them have water and electricity. The camp stands on elevated land bordered by salt marsh creeks. The adjacent creeks are barely visible because the woods are so thick on the edge of the campground. Large live oaks draped in Spanish moss shade the campsites, along with some pines and water oaks. Grass and leaf litter cover the forest floor. A centrally located bathhouse with hot showers serves the campground. For the big rigs 50-amp and 30-amp hookups are available.

RVs and trailers mainly occupy the campground in the winter, with more tent campers during the summer. Davis Bayou fills regularly with snowbirds from January through March. Otherwise sites are generally available, though the place also fills during holiday weekends such as Easter, Memorial Day, and Labor Day. Reservations are not accepted, so you must take your chances during these times. Call the park to get an idea of campground capacity if you are unsure whether to come. Davis Bayou is known for having visitors who return year after year. Fans of the national park system, birders, and many locals call Davis Bayou home for at least a few nights per year.

Human and Natural History

West Ship Island has had a lighthouse for more than 150 years. A brick tower housing a light was first built there in 1853 to protect boats in the shallow Mississippi Sound traveling between Mobile and New Orleans. Erosion forced the erection of a second lighthouse, using the old lighthouse lens, in 1886. Although built of wood, the new structure was strong enough to withstand a hurricane, as lighthouse keeper Dan McColl and his wife found out in 1893 when they hunkered down inside the lighthouse through a storm. Dangers aside, the loneliness and isolation were what drove most lighthouse keepers back to the mainland. The last keeper of the light left in 1955, and later the light was relocated. The attractive white wooden lighthouse tower remained until 1972, when campers accidentally burned it to the ground. The Ship Island Lighthouse was rebuilt but was wiped out by Hurricane Katrina in 2005.

What to Do

The Davis Bayou unit of Gulf Islands National Seashore has modest recreational facilities. Park visitors like to walk and bicycle the quiet roads within Davis Bayou. Two short nature trails offer a more secluded experience. As noted, the park has its own fishing pier, and a boat ramp allows those who have a boat to explore the sloughs and bayous that open to the Gulf. Canoers and kayakers ply the calmer, more protected waters in the park. Weekend interpretive programs are held year-round.

The Live Oaks Bicycle Route leaves Davis Bayou and winds through the back streets of Ocean Springs. You can follow the designated bicycle route signs for 15 miles past old homes, quiet beaches, and museums.

A trip to West Ship Island to see historic Fort Massachusetts is a must for visitors. Rangers lead daily tours when the ferryboat is operating. Take the boardwalk from the bay side of the island a third of a mile to the Gulf side for a primitive island experience. The few island amenities, such as outdoor showers, are on the bay side. A swimming beach overlooks the Gulf and beachcombing can be good. For ferry schedule information, call (866) 466-7386 or visit www.msship.com.

What's Nearby

The towns of Biloxi and Ocean Springs have become vacation destinations with many opportunities for all manner of activities, and the recent rise of coastal casinos has been a big draw. Historic homes in both cities offers touring opportunities. Guided walking tours are given in Ocean Springs, whereas in Biloxi you can take a tour train through the Historic District, downtown, and the Point. One home not to be missed is Beauvoir, the home of the Confederacy's only president, Jefferson Davis. Fishing charters, nature tours, shrimping trips, sailing trips, and more pedestrian offerings such as water parks and miniature golf round out the nearby tourist offerings. However, Hurricane Katrina disrupted the state of affairs here; be patient as the folks of the Magnolia State rebuild their coastline.

Information

Davis Bayou, Gulf Islands National Seashore
1801 Gulf Breeze Parkway
Gulf Breeze, FL 32563
(850) 934-2600
www.nps.gov/guis
Open: Year-round
Sites: 52 water and electric sites
Amenities: Electricity, water, picnic table, upright grill, fire ring
Registration: Self registration at campground office
Facilities: Hot showers, flush toilets, pay phone
Fees: $16 per night if you use electricity; $14 no electricity
Directions: From the intersection of I-110 and US 90 in Biloxi, Mississippi, take US 90 east for 7.7 miles to Park Drive. Turn right on Park Drive and enter the national seashore.

Buccaneer State Park

Bay St. Louis, Mississippi

Buccaneer State Park is located on the western Mississippi Gulf Coast near the historic town of Bay St. Louis. The park was closed for a period after Hurricane Katrina, but the Mississippi Department of Natural Resources vowed to restore it. This is one of the least busy areas of the Magnolia State's coastal region. The park itself is a fine destination, where pines, oaks, and other shade trees provide cover from the southern sun and make for an attractive natural setting. The quality, well-kept campground has sites for RVs and tent campers. And there are some onsite activities, most notable of which is a water park with a large wavepool. Though the park has some limited beachfront, there is plenty of other beachfront nearby for those who want to dig their toes into the sand. As elsewhere on the Mississippi Gulf Coast, nearby options include touring historic homes or gambling at the casinos that have sprung up in this part of the world.

Figure 9. Footprints in the sand near Bucanneer State Park.

The Beach/Coast

The entrance to Buccaneer State Park is just across the two-lane Beach Boulevard from the Gulf. This boulevard runs parallel to the shoreline, and there is some sandy land directly across it from the park entrance. Within the state park the main attraction is its water park with a wavepool and two waterslides. Just east of the park is a large beach area maintained by Hancock County, in which Buccaneer State Park lies. There is also a fishing pier in this direction. Going west along Beach Boulevard, you will see fine historic homes overlooking the Gulf from the landward side of Beach Boulevard. The Gulf side of the road is nothing but sand and is open to the public. Be apprised that parking spots are limited; make sure you park in a legal spot before setting up on the beach. A paved path extends along much of the shoreline, enabling bikers and pedestrians to get around and to access the beach. The Gulf of Mexico extends as far as the eye can see from these beaches. As you approach Bay St. Louis, you will come to the Washington Avenue Pier, a fishing and beach destination open to everyone.

The Campground

This campground is well kept and in an attractive forested setting. A nice level grassy area is complemented by scattered shade trees. The first area, with campsites #1–#25, is by reservation only and has a mix of sun and shade. Two more nearby loops provide RV sites that attract big rigs and pop-ups. Two more quality loops are across the way, then you come to the hub of the campground: an activity building for rainy days, a camp store, two tennis courts, a miniature golf course, basketball court, and wading pool. This setup is very convenient for campers as one can simply walk from the campsites to use any of these facilities.

The back of the campground is my favorite area. It is more shaded and less busy. The Royal Cay Loop has a mix of tall pines and oaks. The primitive tent camping area is in thick woods just off the Royal Cay Loop. A gravel road enters into the woods and here lie many flat spots carpeted with pine needles and leaves. The campsites are not indicated or designated in any way. Just pick your spot. The thick shade comes in handy on hot days. Be apprised that a railroad track runs nearby and you will hear trains, though they did not bother me during my stay. Treasure Cove is the final camping area. It is the best of the designated loop campsites. It borders a grassy wetland but is shaded overhead and has vegetation between sites for good privacy.

Bathhouses are scattered throughout the 209 designated campsites. The campground fills at Easter and over summer holiday weekends. It is during these times that overflow campsites, near the water park, are used. Primitive sites are always available.

Human and Natural History

Choctaw Indians originally claimed the Gulf Coast as home, living in the village of Chicapoula, where Bay St. Louis is today. French explorers first landed here in 1699, establishing the community of Bay St. Louis, which was named for King Louis XIV. French settlement was sparse and Bay St. Louis was handed over to the British after the French and Indian War of the 1760s. Then the land was passed among the British, French, and Spanish before the Americans took full and permanent possession in 1811. The state of Mississippi came to be six years later, and Hancock County soon followed. Bay St. Louis was the county seat. Oddly enough, the town name was changed to Shieldsborough but was later changed back to Bay St. Louis. Its name reflects its history as the oldest community on the Mississippi Gulf Coast.

What to Do

Even though it is mere yards from the tantalizing Gulf shore, Buccaneer's water park is its big draw. The wave pool brings in visitors of all ages, whereas the two waterslides are used by the younger set, and there is a kiddie pool for the very young. Day after day during the summer visitors find a spot along the coast, from the Hancock County Beach eastward all the way to the historic part of Bay St. Louis, and engage in sunning, swimming, and shelling on the stretch of beach adjacent to the park. Anglers enjoy the nearby piers for fishing.

Park activities include hiking on the Pirates' Alley Nature Trail, miniature golf, basketball, tennis, and disc golf (get your discs at the park office). A day use area offers picnicking facilities across Beach Boulevard from the Gulf.

What's Nearby

Old Bay St. Louis is an area on the shore that has been preserved. Restaurants and shops are located in historic buildings. It is fun to stroll around and get a taste of what the Gulf Coast used to be like, and one can also see something of the revitalization efforts following Hurricane Katrina. West Ship Island lies off the coast and is worth a visit to see Fort Massachusetts; on this now primitive island, beachcombing is better than on the mainland. For ferry schedule information, call (866) 466-7386 or visit www.msshipisland.com.

Information

Buccaneer State Park
1150 South Beach Boulevard
Waveland, MS 39576
(228) 467-3822, www.mdwfp.com
Open: Year-round
Sites: 209 developed sites, unlimited primitive sites
Amenities: Developed sites have electricity, water, picnic table, fire ring, lantern post; primitive tents sites have no amenities
Registration: At park office, on the Internet, or by phone
Facilities: Hot showers, flush toilets, laundry, pay phone
Fees: RV sites with water, electricity, and sewer $16 per night; $14 for water and electricity only; primitive tent sites $10
Directions: From I-10 in Mississippi near the Louisiana-Mississippi border take exit 2 to MS 607 south and follow it for 6 miles to reach US 90. Continue on US 90 east to reach Lakeshore Road, which is past a huge standing alligator sign. Turn right on Lakeshore Road and follow it 4.5 miles to reach the Gulf. Turn left here and follow Beach Boulevard 1.5 miles to reach the park, on your left.

Alabama

Gulf State Park
Gulf Shores, Alabama

Hurricane Ivan devastated Gulf State Park and the surrounding coast of Alabama and Florida in 2004. The park was closed for several months. However, during that time Alabama state park personnel and others began restoring, repairing, and upgrading park facilities. You might say the hurricane was a blessing in disguise. I saw the damage firsthand and it was not easy then to view the devastation as any kind of blessing. But visitors coming to the restored Gulf State Park will appreciate the upgraded facilities along with its naturally beautiful white sand beaches overlooking the Gulf of Mexico, sandwiched between the cities of Orange Beach and Gulf Shores. Lakes and woods are located inland and are part of the 6,000 acres of coastal ecosystem protected by the state park. The very large campground, located on the shore of Middle Lake, was also completely redone and attracts visitors year-round.

The Beach/Coast

You will know when you have arrived at Gulf State Park, Alabama's premier Gulf Coast destination: greeting you is a two-mile stretch of shining white beach with beautiful sweeping views of the Gulf. The beach is very wide here and lacks significant dunes. There is plenty of room for thousands of beachgoers to stretch out. A park resort and convention center are at the west end of the property. The Alabama state fishing pier extends into the Gulf nearby. A pavilion with restrooms and cold showers is next to the beach parking area.

Gulf State Park also has two lakes just inland from the beach. These are freshwater lakes despite being so close to the sea. The large Lake Shelby can be seen from AL 180, the road bordering the Gulf, with a picnic area and park building on the Gulf side of the lake. A roped-off swimming area allows visitors to choose salt or fresh water for their aquatic endeavors. Shelby Lake is connected to Middle Lake by a boat canal. The campground overlooks Middle Lake, which has alligators in it—no swimming is allowed. Small boats with motors are allowed on both lakes. Other nearby beach options include Perdido Key State Recreation Area just over the Florida border, Bon Secour National Wildlife Refuge, and Fort Morgan.

The Campground

The campground at Gulf State Park has nearly 500 campsites. To me that would normally be a red flag, but Gulf State Park bucks the trend for two reasons: the campground spreads out widely through the attractive woodland beside Middle Lake, and it received a complete overhaul after Hurricane Ivan. Every campsite was redone, with water, electricity, and sewer hookups installed along with new parking pads. The electric hookups are 50 and 30 amps. Some trees were brought down by the storm, but much of the natural vegetation, primarily pine woods, remains. The campsites by Middle Lake and the boat canal are snapped up first. Numerous camp roads stretch back into the forest away from the lake. Many of the sites are pull-through and others are pull-up sites. Eleven bathhouses are spaced through the campground.

The park has a campers' community house on Middle Lake, along with a nature center, tennis courts, and a camp store. There are some boat slips on Middle Lake for campers. As already indicated, no swimming is allowed on Middle Lake because of the presence of 'gators.

Gulf State Park sees about 95 percent RVs in the winter and about 75 percent during summer. Snowbirds fill the campground by mid-January, due to attractive monthly rates. Business slows down in April and May. The campground is full on summer weekends, but you can usually get a site during the week. Reservations are recommended and can be made a year in advance.

Human and Natural History

Bon Secour National Wildlife Refuge, located west of Gulf Shores, protects some important coastline along Alabama's shore. Dunes rise from the sea and birds stop over on migration. This 7,000-acre preserve, small by national wildlife refuge standards, is a place for loggerhead turtles to nest and for the Alabama beach mouse to make a stand. The piping plover is a rare and solitary shorebird that can be seen here. Bon Secour means "safe harbor" in French, a fitting name for the refuge. It not only protects the coastline and provides recreation opportunities on its five miles of Gulf beaches but also has twelve miles of bayfront. The refuge is located west of Gulf State Park on AL 180.

What to Do

Gulf State Park has one of the best stretches of beach in Alabama, making this the primary draw for visitors. With two miles of beachfront and an ultrawide and level swath of sand, you will have no problem finding room for your lounger and umbrella. Lake Shelby offers freshwater swimming and fishing. The Alabama state pier extends into the Gulf, if you wish to fish for saltwater species.

Running through the woods behind the campground is a series of intertwined nature trails. If you prefer wheeled travel, bring a bike or rent one at the camp store. The campground roads offer plenty of places to pedal—it's a mile and a half from one end of the campground to the other, not counting the side roads. If you bring your clubs, you can play the park golf course.

What's Nearby

Perhaps you have heard the saying: "Damn the torpedoes, full speed ahead!" This was uttered by Admiral David Farragut during the 1864 Battle of Mobile Bay as the Confederacy fired on the admiral's Union gunships from Fort Morgan, near Gulf State Park. The fort, occupied by the Rebels, was besieged by Farragut and ultimately surrendered. Today this scenic locale overlooks Mobile Bay and is on the National Register of Historic Places. Fort Morgan was originally erected to protect the valuable port of Mobile. After the Civil War, the United States continued to use the fort until it was turned over to the State of Alabama as a historic site. To visit the fort, go west from Gulf Shores on AL 180 and enjoy the views and habitats that attract both history buffs and migratory birds.

Information

Gulf State Park
22050 Campground Road
Gulf Shores, AL, 36542
(800) 252-7275, www.alapark.com; reservations (800) 252-7275
Sites: 494

Open: Year-round

Amenities: Picnic table, grill, water, electricity, sewer

Registration: By phone or at park entrance booth

Facilities: Hot showers, flush toilets, pay phone, camp store

Fees: $14–$24 per night; reduced rates for weekly or monthly stays and during winter

Directions: Take exit 37 from I-65 to AL 287 (Rabun Road, County Road 47). Turn left onto AL 287 and continue on it for approximately 1 mile. Continue onto AL 59 South and travel approximately 50 miles. Turn left onto AL 180 East (Fort Morgan Road) and travel less than a mile. Continue onto AL 135 (Fort Morgan Road) and travel less than a mile to the park entrance.

Florida

Fort Pickens, Gulf Islands National Seashore
Pensacola, Florida

The Fort Pickens area is the crown jewel of the Gulf Islands National Seashore system. This federally protected seashore covers several coastal areas in Florida and Mississippi. Fort Pickens is located on the western tip of Santa Rosa Island—a seven-mile stretch of preserved barrier island that features a fascinating historic fort. This area was devastated by Hurricane Ivan in 2004, but hard work has brought the park back up to speed.

Many lives have passed through the fort, which has been through numerous phases from 1829 to 1947, when it was finally deactivated. Now it is part of a national park where you can walk the beach, ride your bike, and explore the island at will. The miles and miles of pristine beach inspire people to return time and again, to feel the ocean breeze and absorb the beauty of this preserved stretch of shore. The campground is spacious, with sites available nearly every day of the year. It makes a good base for other attractions nearby on Santa Rosa Island, at Santa Rosa Sound, and in downtown Pensacola.

The Beach/Coast

Bring your sunglasses to Fort Pickens—the white sand will blind you. Many seaside stretches have little in the way of vegetation. The beach extends westward all the way to the tip of the island, where a channel cuts through—the only entrance to Pensacola Bay. As you continue around the perimeter of the narrow island, Pensacola Bay and the naval shipyards come into view. Fort Pickens is just inland, and a few other park service buildings are in the area. The bay side of the seashore has both marsh and beach environments. The protected coastline continues for seven miles back to the park border.

As you look inland from the Fort Pickens area, notice a low wall a few hundred yards distant from the fort itself. That was a seawall constructed in 1907 after a devastating hurricane hit the fort. The wall is now pretty far from the shore. Next, look at Fort Pickens. Imagine it being just a hundred yards from the ship channel. When the fort was constructed in 1829, that's how far it was from the shore.

Santa Rosa Island, like all Gulf barrier islands, is migrating westward. Winds come in primarily from the southeast, pounding the shore and pushing sand westward. Sand builds on the western ends of the barrier islands while being stripped away from the eastern ends. Hurricanes like Ivan in 2004 can accelerate the process dramatically.

The Campground

Fort Pickens has a spacious campground with more than 200 sites located in the wooded interior of the island. Pines and a few live oaks shade the campsites. Having little understory vegetation lends an open feel to the campground. The grass beneath the trees is always mown, making it seem as if you are camping on a lawn. The bathroom facilities are clean but antiquated. Hot showers are available.

The campground is divided into five loops. Loop A is located separate from the rest and paved parking areas make this the preferred loop for the RV crowd. The other four loops are all connected. Loop B is next to some dunes and has hills and old military ruins to break it up. Loop C is in an area of tall pine trees. Loop D has the most spacious sites, including a few under some wide-spreading live oaks. Loop E has some sites looking out over Pensacola Bay.

Overall the campground is clean and well kept. Some of the sites are a little close together, but there are plenty of appealing ones. You'll have your pick during the quiet winter season. Business picks up during spring. Summer weekends are the busiest times, though by evening all campsites may be filled on any summer day. So get your campsite early. Fall is a great time to visit—good weather and no crowds. Overnight stays are limited to thirty calendar days per year and no more than fourteen days between March 1 and Labor Day.

Human and Natural History

The construction of Fort Pickens was begun in 1829 and took five years. To hold the massive weight of the bricks and cannons an ingenious system of arches spread the weight over the packed sand foundation. The masonry forts could fire their cannons onto wooden ships and expect little threat in return. With this fort in place, no enemy ever dared attack. That was the idea behind the forts: to have them there as a deterrent, so that each could be manned by a skeleton crew rather requiring than a large and costly standing army.

The only action at Fort Pickens came during the Civil War when Confederates occupied nearby Forts McRee and Barrancas. The Union held Pickens; cannon fire was exchanged. The only casualties were three cannon operators hit when lucky southerners fired a cannonball that came through a small window in Fort Pickens.

In later years the fort went through many alterations. The most visible is Battery Pensacola, built in 1898 to house more cannon emplacements. Fort Pickens was manned until after World War II, undergoing more modernizations, including the erection of many battery installations around the fort. The fort became part of the Gulf Islands National Seashore in 1971.

What to Do

With more than 14 miles of beach, you can run your toes in the sand and look for shells until your legs ache. Boardwalks lead to the most popular beach, Langdon Beach, just across the road from the campground. Other beach access points are along Fort Pickens Road. You can swim anywhere except in the shipping channel. The Blackbird Marsh Nature Trail makes a little loop near the campground, exploring another coastal environment. The Florida Trail, a footpath, passes through the national seashore to reach its northern terminus at the fort after meandering 1,100 miles from South Florida. A fishing pier is helpful to anglers, though surf fishing is both popular and productive.

By all means take the driving tour of all the fortified batteries on the island, but the best tour of all is the ranger-led tour of the actual fort itself. It lasts an hour, beginning at 2:00 p.m. daily during high season, with less frequency during winter. A self-guided tour is better than nothing, but the ranger can answer all those questions that come up.

What's Nearby

The main attractions nearby are the Naval Live Oaks area of the Gulf Islands National Seashore, the Pensacola Bay Fishing Bridge, and historic downtown Pensacola. Naval Live Oaks is an area established by John Quincy Adams as an experimental tree farm to grow live oaks for use in ship building. It consists today of 1,300 acres of natural coast on the mainland, harboring many plant and animal communities, including live oaks.

Trails runs through the Naval Live Oaks unit, one of them following the route of the old Pensacola–St. Augustine Road, constructed in 1824. The main visitor center for the Gulf Islands National Seashore is here also. It has picnic shelters and an observation deck, and there is bayside shoreline to explore.

Cast a line from the Pensacola Bay fishing bridge to catch sea trout, king mackerel, bluefish, and jacks. A convenient fishing camp store is located at the end of the bridge. The Seville Historic District in downtown Pensacola has old museums, churches, and houses you can tour. The historic district visitor center is at the Tivoli House on Bayfront Parkway. The Civil War Soldiers Museum is also located in downtown Pensacola.

Information

Fort Pickens, Gulf Islands National Seashore
1801 Gulf Breeze Parkway
Gulf Breeze, FL 32563
(850) 934-2600, www.nps.gov/guis; reservations (800) 365-2267, www.reservations.nps.gov
Open: Year-round
Sites: 200
Amenities: Water, electricity, picnic table, fire ring
Registration: At campground registration building
Facilities: Hot showers, flush toilets, laundry, pay phone, camp store
Fees: $20 per night
Directions: From Pensacola, drive south on State Road 399 for 7 miles to Pensacola Beach, passing over a toll bridge. In Pensacola Beach, turn right on Fort Pickens Road, which takes you right to the Fort Pickens unit of the Gulf Islands National Seashore.

Henderson Beach State Recreation Area
Destin, Florida

Would you like to do some beach camping in a $13 million campground? It must be a great place. The $13 million was for the land alone, not counting the park infrastructure, and that was back in 1981; imagine what the place is worth now. This prime parcel of beach is located in the heart of fast-growing Destin, Florida, where the word is that land prices are marked with a pencil because they rise so rapidly. However, anyone can enjoy this fine property with an excellent campground for a mere twenty-one dollars per night. The town of Destin is just outside the park gate, which allows for a mix of nature and more urban pursuits. I used to vacation in Destin as a child, and the place is barely recognizable as what I knew. This rapid development makes Henderson Beach all the more valuable.

The Beach/Coast

The Henderson family sold their land to the state to ensure that it would be preserved in its natural state to allow public use of this rolling beachfront with sugar-white sand backed by dunes. The park protects slightly more than a mile of beach frontage. On the west side tall condos tower over the Gulf.

Figure 10. Looking out on the white sands and alluring waters of Henderson Beach.

More structures and beachfront abut the east side. In the middle lies Henderson Beach, the most natural beach area in Destin. The west side of the beach has the primary day use area, with two large pavilions, cold showers, restrooms, and covered picnic areas. Boardwalks drop over the dunes and onto the beautiful white beach. The gentle curve of the shoreline leads to a boardwalk on the east end of the beach. This is known as the Camper's Beach, since the boardwalk leads up to the park campground. Other nearby beach areas include Topsail Hill State Preserve, a state-owned property that went for $100 million!

The Campground

Henderson Beach has one of the newer campgrounds in the Florida state park system. State officials have learned a lot over the years and put it to use here. They made preserving the natural setting the first priority and integrated the campground into the landscape rather than the other way around. The place is a beautiful woodland of wind-sculpted sand pines, with attendant lower vegetation such as palmetto, yaupon, and wax myrtle growing thick. The 60 campsites are spread over four loops. Loops A and B are grouped together, sharing a bathhouse. These campsites all have water and electricity. A special amenity is a clothesline for hanging those wet towels. Most sites allow full-size RVs, and some are pull-through sites, which make parking your rig easier. However, be aware that absolutely as much vegetation as possible is kept between the sites; it makes for great campsite privacy but can mean parking is a tight squeeze. Loops C and D are at the end of the campground road. They also share a bathhouse. These sites are all worthy of a night of beach camping. A trail leads from each camping area to the boardwalk accessing the beach.

Henderson Beach is very popular. It fill on most weekends and during the week at warm times and in pleasant weather. Snowbirds are putting increasing campsite pressure on the place in winter, though a ranger told me January might be the slowest time. For peace of mind, reservations are strongly recommended at any time of year.

Human and Natural History

Nearby Topsail Hill State Preserve, east of Henderson Beach, has an amazing three miles of Gulf frontage. This area has an extensive dune ecosystem and is still in a wild state. Some of the older dunes are now vegetated beachside hills. An RV resort has been developed onsite.

Topsail Hill was formed from ten purchases made over the period 1991 to 1996. Think about its high price when you squiggle your toes through the sand. It was a good thing the State bought the property when it did, given the way land values on Florida's coast continue to rise; eventually, it seems, every inch of privately owned coastline is going to be developed. Topsail Hill is special in another way: it contains two highly unusual lakes. Lake Morris and Lake Campbell, immediately behind the seaside dunes, are reputedly the closest lakes to any coast that do not have saltwater intrusion.

What to Do

The action at Henderson Beach is all about the Gulf frontage. Most people like to hang out on the gorgeous white beach, swim and sun and walk the surf line and look at other people. Since the state land amounts to only 208 acres, other options are limited. A nature trail extends three quarters of a mile through the dunes, where the coastal beach dune ecosystem is explained via interpretive signs. It's a quick way to get up to speed on what lives in this harsh environment. And you can feel practically *royal* about that knowledge—this and the Nearby Topsail Hill State Preserve hiking trail are probably the most expensive land over which most of us will ever hike.

What's Nearby

Destin is on its way to becoming a megalopolis lining the entire local coastline. Directly beyond the gates of Henderson Beach State Recreation Area, you are in town, with every kind of store and tourist activity you can imagine. My childhood memory of it scarcely extends beyond the beach itself and perhaps an ice cream cone. Now you can buy, eat, ride, and experience just about anything here.

Information

Henderson Beach State Recreation Area
1700 Emerald Coast Parkway
Destin, FL 32541
(850) 837-7550, www.floridastateparks.org; camping reservations (800) 326-3521, www.reserveamerica.com

Open: Year-round
Sites: 60
Amenities: Picnic table, fire ring, clothesline, water, electricity
Registration: By phone or Internet
Facilities: Hot showers, flush toilets, laundry
Fees: $21 per night
Directions: Henderson State Recreation Area is located in the city of Destin, 1.5 miles west of FL 293, the Mid Bay Bridge. It is on the south side of US 98.

Grayton Beach State Recreation Area

Santa Rosa Beach, Florida

Grayton Beach is consistently rated among the top ten beaches in the United States, which makes a clear case for visiting this state recreation area. And it deserves its status as one of the best. Sugar-white sand contrasts with the clear green waters of the Gulf of Mexico. This part of Florida is known as the Emerald Coast. But there's more here than just a sandy shoreline. The beach rises into rolling dunes, splotched with wind-sculpted vegetation that slowly descends into smaller secondary dunes and finally into Western Lake, just on the mainland side of the big dunes.

Grayton Beach State Recreation Area stretches across County Road 30A with more woodland, which melds into Point Washington State Forest. This forest land provides other recreation opportunities, especially for hikers and bikers. And just a short drive away are two other fantastic beach acquisitions owned by the state for public use—Camp Helen and Deer Lake. These beaches will make you wonder why you didn't come this way sooner.

The Beach/Coast

Grayton Beach extends for a mile along the Gulf. A boardwalk runs from the parking area over the dunes to access the beach. As you walk the boardwalk, look both ways and see how salt spray and wind have worked live oaks and myrtle oaks into thickets that rise and fall with the undulation of the dunes.

Figure 11. Grayton Beach.

These great dunes are constantly being altered. Another boardwalk leads to the Grayton Beach Nature Trail, which heads inland. Western Lake has some decent shoreline of its own. In many places, especially near the campground, the salt marsh gives way to sand, forming a lake beach. Here you can access the clear, brackish waters of the lake.

Camp Helen has a wide beach. Follow the path from the park entrance over a small inlet of Lake Powell and around a dune area to a beach with an old pier. The sand extends a good two hundred yards to the dunes. The brackish water of Phillips Inlet splits the beach apart.

Cross an extensive area of dunes to reach Deer Lake Beach. This beach is less well known and more secluded but has only around a third of a mile of Gulf waterfront. A boardwalk leads to the beach. There is a picnic shelter near the parking area.

The Campground

Grayton Beach has a well laid-out and perfectly sized 36-site campground next to Western Lake. Rich vegetation enhances most campsites. Pine trees provide shade overhead. Sand live oak, yaupon, palmetto, and turkey oak have grown into thickets that form privacy barriers between the campsites. Yet this growth isn't so suffocating that an RV can't pull in and out or that tent campers can't spread their gear about.

A bathhouse stands in the center of the camping loop. Trails through the thickety vegetation to allow campers to reach the bathhouse without cutting through campsites. Short pathways have also been cut from the loop road to access the beach of Western Lake, since only eight of the campsites overlook Western Lake and have lake beach access paths of their own. Those eight sites are desirable, for they overlook not only the lake but also the beach dunes beyond Western Lake.

On the far side of the loop from Western Lake, the campsites are bigger and more open. They back up to a younger pine and turkey oak forest. Campers driving bigger RVs will be more comfortable in these sites. Tenters will want sites closer to the lake to maximize the benefits of any breezes blowing.

The busy season at Grayton Beach starts in March and lasts through the middle of September. Expect a full house every day. Snowbirds also keep the campground busy during cooler months. Park personnel "most definitely" recommend making reservations. The publicity of having one of the best beaches in America has its price.

Figure 12. Camp Helen State Park is located near Grayton Beach.

Human and Natural History

Luckily for us, Florida has been acquiring public beach land for some time. Grayton Beach came first. The Deer Lake tract comprises nearly 2,000 acres, but most of it is on the mainland side of CR 30A, although the actual Deer Lake is on the beach side of the road. This tract is nonetheless valuable for preserving oceanside habitat and as a development buffer, and it does have some beach frontage.

Camp Helen sits high on a hill overlooking Lake Powell and the Gulf. It was first a development that failed, then an employee retreat for a company from Alabama. It has cabins, cottages, and an old lodge on beautiful grounds grown up with live oaks, hickories, and palm trees. Beyond the lodge are Phillips Inlet and the rather large beach area.

What to Do

The highly rated beach at Grayton is the main attraction of this recreation area. Sunbathers and swimmers gather here in the warmer months. Fishermen can enjoy Grayton Beach also. Surf fishing in the Gulf for saltwater species is enjoyed year-round. Western Lake has both freshwater and saltwater species. There is a boat ramp at Western Lake and canoes are available for rental. Park explorers can hike the Grayton Beach Nature Trail so as to explore the dunes without harming them. The trail also traverses pine flatwoods, then crosses the dunes on a boardwalk and completes a loop via the beach. It's a Grayton Beach sampler.

What's Nearby

The multiple state beaches in the area offer many chances to explore. They are all close. Get directions at Grayton Beach. My initial sighting of the beach at Deer Lake was memorable. I followed a narrow footpath through dense woods and crossed a small, fairly high saddle between two dunes. The beach opened up before me. Rolling sand—some vegetated, some not—gave way to gentle Gulf waters stretching as far as the eye could see. Deer Lake is just a few miles east of Grayton Beach on CR 30A.

If you like a little history and a quaint lodge with your beach, visit Camp Helen. The park has beach frontage for swimming and sunbathing. A figure-eight hiking trail explores the grounds of this 1940s era vacation spot.

Hikers and bikers may want to check out the Eastern Lake Trail in the Point Washington State Forest just a few miles away. It has a system of three interlocking double-track loop trails of 3, 5, and 10 miles. These trails wind through sandhills, scrub, cypress ponds, and wet prairie. A trip to yet another state holding, Eden State Gardens, is worth your while. The wealthy owner of a lumber company built a fine large home with well-manicured grounds and gardens. His daughter left it to the state. It is located near the town of Port Washington.

Information

Grayton Beach State Recreation Area
357 Main Park Road
Santa Rosa Beach, FL 32549
(850) 231-4210, www.floridastateparks.org; camping reservations (800) 326-3521, www.reserveamerica.com
Open: Year-round
Sites: 36

Amenities: Picnic table, fire ring, water, electricity
Registration: By phone or Internet
Facilities: Hot showers, flush toilets, pay phone
Fees: $19 per night
Directions: From Fort Walton Beach, drive east on US 98 for 18 miles to County Road 30A. Head east on CR 30A for nine miles. Grayton Beach State Recreation Area will be on your right.

St. Andrews State Recreation Area

Panama City, Florida

St. Andrews is one of the busiest parks in the state. That's because it lies just a short bridge away from Panama City. The 176-site campground, the largest in the state park system, can be congested during the warmer months, but be patient and you will find the St. Andrews experience rewarding. It is an opportunity to camp on a slice of natural Florida surrounded by a thriving tourist town, a double dose of Panhandle fun.

Panama City is just a short drive away, offering everything from fine dining to the tacky tourist traps that have given the town its dubious nickname: the "Redneck Riviera." But St. Andrews is a worthy destination in its own right. The natural confines of the park contain a nice stretch of beach, clear blue water, high sand dunes, marsh, and a barrier island worth a boat ride. Just remember to make camping reservations as early as you can.

Figure 13. Beachcombers walk the shore at St. Andrews State Recreation Area.

The Beach/Coast

Urban development can't get any closer to St. Andrews than it has already come, for the recreation area is surrounded on three sides by water, which is great news for beach lovers. The sugar-white sand forms large dunes on the Gulf side of the park. A rock jetty extends into the Gulf and helps maintain the depth of the channel that is the main entrance to the port of Panama City. Sandy Point extends into St. Andrews Bay. The third water-bound side of the park lies along Grand Lagoon, with smaller stretches of sand and calmer waters.

Most swimming and beachcombing take place on the Gulf side of St. Andrews. No matter how big the crowds, there is plenty of beach for everyone to find a spot. The jetty lures in fishermen. Behind the jetty is a pool of calm water for those not willing to tackle the waves coming in from the Gulf.

If you want the experience of walking a deserted, unpopulated beach, go to Shell Island, 700 acres of protected real Florida stretching for seven miles. Shell Island is located just across the channel from St. Andrews, easily visible from the jetty. The island supports deer and other wildlife, which divide their time between St. Andrews, Shell Island, and the woods of nearby Tyndall Air Force Base. They do this by swimming the short stretches of ocean that separate the three places.

The Campground

Having the largest campground in the state park system and being next to a popular tourist destination are factors that present challenges for the personnel at St. Andrews. It can get busy. Two defined campgrounds lie side by side. The Pine Grove Campground has 76 sites stretched around three loops. As the name suggests, tall pine trees sway over the camp area. An understory of palmetto breaks up the campsites. Seventeen campsites face Grand Lagoon. Some feature beachfront; others have sawgrass growing between them and the water. Two bathhouses serve Pine Grove. The Lagoon Campground has 100 sites on either side of Campers Drive. One side of the drive backs up to Grand Lagoon, and the other side backs up to high ancient sand dunes. Generally speaking the sites are smaller and closer together. The area also is beneath many pines. Smaller oaks grow here and there, but the farther you go toward the channel, the more open campsites become until there is no cover between sites. Thirty-two campsites are directly on Grand Lagoon.

This campground is full almost constantly during the warm season. Winters are getting busier. Reservations are highly recommended.

Human and Natural History

Have you heard the story of Teddy the Hermit? He was the park's first "camper." Actually, when it became park property he had been living there since 1929. Before coming to St. Andrews he'd been living on his boat in a nearby marina. But in September of '29 a hurricane struck. Teddy fled inland and returned to find his boat missing.

He came upon the boat near where campsite #15 is today. The craft was in bad shape, but Teddy resolved to repair it. Meanwhile, he made a temporary little shack to live in. Alas, the boat was beyond repair, so Teddy made his shack near campsite #101 more livable. Teddy, his cats, and chickens homesteaded on St. Andrews. He hand-dug a well for fresh water. For cash he sold fish to a local market, and he would go to town every now and then for goods he couldn't get from nature.

In 1946 the state of Florida acquired the land and gave Teddy, then sixty-four years old, a lifetime lease. Park visitors would go and see him. It is said that he was the main attraction in the early days. He passed away near his cabin in 1954.

What to Do

Everybody loves a beautiful beach, and St. Andrews has one. High dunes make for good vantage points. Or you can walk right next to the waves. Summer finds many swimmers and snorkelers, especially around Shell Island. Divers explore wrecks farther out to sea. Fishing is popular here, and understandably so. With opportunities as diverse as surf fishing, a Gulf fishing pier, jetty fishing, and a bay fishing pier, something is biting year-round. Catches often include redfish, flounder, Spanish mackerel, king mackerel, bluefish, and grouper.

For those who want to venture into the water, canoes and kayaks are available for rent. There is a boat launch if you have you own watercraft. You can also take a shuttle to nearby Shell Island. This is a favorite with most visitors to St. Andrews, especially in the glass-bottomed boats. The shuttles operate during the warmer months and are fairly inexpensive. Walking the beach on Shell Island is worth the price of a shuttle ride.

St. Andrews has quality interpretive trails and programs. Be sure to check out the turpentine still, and then walk the Heron Pond Pine Flatwoods Trail. It's less than a mile in length yet packs in a good overview of beach ecology. The same goes for the Gator Lake Trail—you learn a lot in a short distance. But if you actually want to see an alligator, go to the Buttonwood Marsh. From the overlook at this freshwater marsh, alligators are often spotted.

What's Nearby

Panama City and Panama City Beach are tourist destinations for thousands coming down from all over the South and beyond. Local attractions fit almost everyone's taste and budget. Gulf World features a marine show with dolphins, sharks, and other ocean creatures. Six acres of fun are at Shipwreck Island, a water park with rides, slides, and other wet escapades. Miracle Strip Amusement Park offers over thirty rides that are a little drier than those at Shipwreck Island. Bungee jumps, miniature golf, and go-cart rides round out the entertainment. Visitors can also enjoy a range of ocean activities near St. Andrews—boating, sailing, charter fishing, scuba diving, and riding personal watercraft.

Information

St. Andrews State Recreation Area
4607 State Park Lane
Panama City, FL 32408-7323
(850) 233-5140, www.floridastateparks.org; camping reservations (800) 326-3521, www.reserveamerica.com
Open: Year-round
Sites: 176
Amenities: Picnic table, fire ring, electricity, water
Registration: By phone or Internet
Facilities: Hot showers, flush toilets, pay phone, laundry
Fees: $24 per night
Directions: From Panama City, drive west on US 98, cross the bridge over West Bay, and continue a short distance to County Road 3031. Turn left on CR 3031 and follow it four miles to CR 392. Turn left on CR 392, which shortly goes right into St. Andrews State Recreation Area.

St. George Island State Park

Apalachicola, Florida

St. George is one of the largest barrier islands on Florida's Gulf Coast. The most easterly 2,000 acres are where beaches, sand dunes, and pine trees guard Apalachicola Bay, which lies between St. George Island and the mainland.

Upon entering the park, the first thing you'll notice is the blinding white sand. The beach rises from the emerald ocean waters. Then, where sea oats can grab a foothold, dunes begin, which meld into a pine forest. Beyond the forest lie a narrow beach and the rich waters of Apalachicola Bay. Ponds and grasses dot the island interior, breaking up the woods.

Across the bay is the town of Apalachicola, an old town of the South where most folks make their living from the sea. Marine fare culled from the bay is sold on the waterfront. Farther inland are the ruins of Fort Gadsden, surrounded by the half-million acres of the Apalachicola National Forest. All this is easily accessible from the sun-splashed campground on St. George.

The Beach/Coast

There are nine miles of undeveloped beaches to explore within the park. To see how valuable this land is, check the prices of the beach homes leading up to the park. And you'll see why—rolling dunes yield to sugar-white beaches and then clear Gulf waters extending to the horizon. It's a short walk from

Figure 14. The hiking trail at St. George Island State Park. Photo by Doug Alderson.

several auto pullovers to the land's edge, where storms scatter shells. There are two primary beach access points with covered picnic areas, restrooms, and outdoor showers to cleanse the salty water from your skin. A boardwalk traverses the dunes between the parking area and the beach. Less developed beach accesses are scattered along the main park road.

The bayside beaches are smaller, with less wind and waves but more solitude and potentially more bugs. Boats are seen in the bay, and the trees of the mainland form the skyline. The eastern beaches of the park are very remote. There are three ways to explore them. Hikers can follow the five-mile fire road to the East End, where sand, sea, and sky merge, or one can beachcomb one's way along the Gulf. Adventurous fishermen in four-wheel-drive vehicles can purchase a special permit at the ranger station and drive to the East End. The fire-road trail is also open to bicyclists.

The Campground

The campground lies four miles from the park entrance in the interior of the island, behind some rather large dunes. But it's not so far that you can't hear the surf crash against the shoreline. The 60 sites are spread along a narrow oval. Erect your tent on the grassy floor and park your rig on the crushed oyster shells. Water and electricity are available at every site. Two fully equipped restrooms with showers serve the camping loop.

Most of the campsites extend outward from the loop and are separated by brush that offers some decent privacy for your campsite. Some sites are more open than others. The first half of the loop has smaller campsites that back up to dense vegetation. These are better for tent campers. RV enthusiasts like the sites on the second half of the loop, which are larger and more open with plenty of room to maneuver a house on wheels.

Slash pines are interspersed throughout the campground and offer a little shade. A few smaller oaks offer some shelter from the sun, but around noon the campground gets a whipping from Old Sol. A sun shelter can come in handy here. No matter where you camp, store your food properly; the raccoons are brazen daylight camp robbers and beggars.

From September to February St. George is pretty quiet, but expect a full campground at Thanksgiving and Christmas. Next, spring breakers from up North fill the place up. You can sometimes find a spot on weekdays in the summer, but expect a full house on weekends.

Human and Natural History

St. George is a Gulf barrier island that forms the southern edge of Apalachic-ola Bay. It is 20 miles long and only a mile wide at its widest point. Formed 5,000 years ago, the island was occupied on only seasonally until the early 1900s. Then the turpentining industry came to milk the island's slash pines early in the twentieth century. You can still see evidence of turpentining on many park pine trees along the interior island trail. Black vertical barkless areas with V-shaped scars show where incisions were made in the tree in win-ter for a galvanized metal gutter. A container was placed below the gutter, and in summer resin would flow into the container, known as a "gerty cup." A gerty cup was a special kind of clay pot. The pine resin would be distilled into oil of turpentine, which was used for explosives, in detergents, and in shipbuilding.

What to Do

Sunbathing and beachcombing are the two most popular activities on St. George. Swimmers dot the ocean in summer. Be advised that there are no lifeguards on the beaches here. Hikers have three good trails from which to choose. The fire road leading to the East End extends five miles one way, so be sure to bring water. Two other trails lead from the campground. The 2.5-mile trail to the primitive campground winds through the center of the piney interior and ends at Gap Point. The soft tones of the trees and brush give your eyes a break from the blinding white beaches. Another trail leads a little over a mile to the north side of the island and overlooks the bay. Bicyclists pedal the quiet road along the island.

You can fish in the surf or the bay. Many people use frozen shrimp to catch flounder and Spanish mackerel. The bay side is said to be productive for red-fish and sea trout. Two bayside boat ramps offer canoers, kayakers, and motor boaters access to the sea.

What's Nearby

A trip to nearby Apalachicola is mandatory for St. George visitors. If you like fresh seafood, as in just off the boat, get some from one of the many waterfront markets in the fishing village. The restored historic district is fun to walk around. Tasteful clothing, gift, and antique shops inhabit the brick buildings, along with a few restaurants and galleries.

You can visit the home of John Gorrie, inventor of the ice machine, and a museum in his honor is just around the corner. He created the ice machine to cool rooms and to prevent malaria. You might call it primitive air conditioning. A little farther inland on Florida Highway 65 is the Fort Gadsden historic site. Built by the Spanish in 1814 beside the Apalachicola River, it later fell into British hands until Andrew Jackson wrestled Florida away from the British and Seminoles. Later the Confederate Army occupied the fort. This site is surrounded by the half-million-acre Apalachicola National Forest, with a network of trails and rivers to keep any outdoor enthusiast busy.

Information

St. George Island State Park
1900 E. Gulf Beach Drive
St. George Island, FL 32328
(850) 927-2111, www.floridastateparks.org; camping reservations (800) 326-3521, www.reserveamerica.com
Open: Year-round
Sites: 60
Amenities: Picnic table, fire ring, water, electricity
Registration: By phone, Internet, or at park entrance booth
Facilities: Hot showers, flush toilets, pay phone
Fees: $19 per night
Directions: From Apalachicola, drive east on US 98 and cross John Gorrie Memorial Bridge. Turn right on County Road 300 and cross St. George Sound to St. George Island. Then turn left on Gulf Beach Drive and follow it for 4 miles to the entrance of St. George Island State Park.

St. Joseph Peninsula State Park
Port St. Joe, Florida

A beachside wilderness area containing the highest sand dunes in Florida, located right on the Gulf—could this be? Yes, this wilderness preserve, two fine camping loops, white sand beaches, and the massive dunes are all part of St. Joseph Peninsula State Park. Located about 50 miles southeast of Panama City, this park is on a narrow spit of land jutting out into the sea. The Gulf of Mexico is to the west. The waters of St. Joseph Bay lie between the 2,516-acre park and the mainland. Miles of sugar-white beaches line the perimeter of the forested peninsula. The park has been unobtrusively developed. You'll appreciate the amenities—marina, camp store and bathhouses—knowing that no development is allowed in the wilderness preserve at the end of the peninsula.

The Beach/Coast

St. Joe, surrounded on three sides by water, has far more beach than it has people. The blinding white beaches are backed with striking sand dunes rolling the length of the peninsula. There are three primary Gulf beach access areas and two primary bay access areas. The main beach is near the small marina, where the peninsula is only about 100 yards wide. Cross the dunes on a boardwalk and the Gulf opens before you. To your left lies the

Figure 15. Brown pelicans dive into the water at St. Joseph Peninsula State Park. Photo by Doug Alderson.

world beyond the borders of the park and to your right are miles of protected beach, where the blue ocean, white sand, and tall dunes meld into the distance.

Access trails lead to the beach from the camping areas. The access to St. Joseph Bay is from the Bay Trail, which leaves from the picnic area. The beach along the bay is smaller and narrower than on the Gulf. The forest grows nearly to the water in spots. The bay is shallow and you can wade far from shore, exploring the wildlife-rich body of water. Horseshoe crab skeletons litter the shoreline. This side of St. Joe is quieter and less windy, though the view of the mainland tarnishes the "deserted island" effect. The other bay access area is on the Coastal Hammock Trail, which starts near the park entrance.

The Campground

The two campgrounds at St. Joe offer quite different atmospheres. The 59-site Gulf Breeze Campground, more open and oriented toward RVs, is located between a marsh and the sand dunes. It is closer to the beach than Shady Pines Campground. Smatterings of pine and palm trees offer some shade. The ocean is just over the dunes, so you can clearly hear the waves lapping the shore and feel the Gulf breeze. Campers have a single bathhouse for their convenience. Roads bisecting the loop allow RV traffic to move safely and freely.

Shady Pines Campground is located in the forest interior. Longleaf pines, coastal live oaks, and sabal palms shade the 51-site loop, which doesn't catch the ocean breeze as the other loop does. Two fully equipped comfort stations serve this camp area. Campsite privacy is well provided by a dense understory of palmetto and yaupon rising high between the sites. This loop is fully electrified, though many of the sites are too thickly wooded to accommodate a big rig.

Some sites are a little on the small side, and a few have low spots that could prove a regrettable choice during a rainstorm. No matter where you camp, store your food properly—the raccoons are notorious bandits.

The campground is busy during spring break. Scallopers and families can fill the campground during summer. Warm days and cool nights lure some campers here in fall. Winter offers more solitude, though Gulf Breeze Campground can be filled with snowbirds.

Human and Natural History

St. Joe occupies the end of an L-shaped peninsula that extends first west and then north into the Gulf of Mexico. It protects the mainland from the direct wrath of the sea. Several types of plant communities can be found here. The older interior dunes are covered in sand pine scrub, while pine flatwoods occupy more level areas. Fresh and salt marshes dot the woodland. Sea oats stabilize the huge dunes.

Indians first occupied this spit. They reaped the undersea gardens of St. Joseph Bay. Later the family of T. H. Stone ran cattle on the peninsula. Just prior to World War II the Stone family sold their land to the U.S. Army for use as a training facility. Nowadays an Air Force installation and an ever-increasing number of beach houses occupy the first few miles of the peninsula. Then the 2,516-acre state park begins, where loggerhead, green, and leatherback sea turtles come ashore to lay their eggs. St. Joe is on the flyway route for spring and fall bird migration. More than 247 species have been recorded here.

What to Do

St. Joe has plenty to offer active campers and beach enthusiasts. Sunbathers have miles of beaches ideal for relaxing and escaping the daily grind. Shelling is productive on both beaches, but especially on the bay side of the park. Scalloping brings back visitors year after year. Fishermen can surf cast for a variety of fish in the Gulf or wade the flats in the shallow bay for sea trout.

Boaters can enjoy the waters no matter what size their craft. The park marina offers docking and launch facilities for larger boats. Canoes are for rent but can only be used in the bay, weather permitting. A canoe or kayak is a great way to explore the preserve. Paddle along the shore of the protected bay, beach your craft, and explore at will.

Birdwatchers can be found throughout the park. The wilderness preserve, covering 1,650 acres at the tip of the peninsula, can be enjoyed by boat or on foot. Walk the wilderness one of three ways: via the Gulf beach, the more difficult bay beach, or the seven-mile interior fire road. Other fire roads split off the main one and lead to either the Gulf or the bay. If you follow the central fire road to its end, you come out on the bay just short of the peninsula point. Follow the beach around to the large sandy point and see where the Gulf meets the bay.

What's Nearby

Other outdoor attractions nearby include the St. Vincent Island National Wildlife Refuge. St. Vincent Island and nearby Pig Island are accessible only by boat. Call (850) 229-1065 for ferry information. About forty miles northeast is the vast Apalachicola National Forest. Highlights include a portion of the Florida National Scenic Trail and some great freshwater canoeing streams, such as Kennedy Creek and Owl Creek. The national forest extends across half a million acres of trees, trails, and rivers that offer a variety of outdoor experiences.

Information

St. Joseph Peninsula State Park
8899 Cape San Blas Road
Port St. Joe, FL 32456
(850) 227-1327, www.floridastateparks.org, camping reservations (800) 326-3521, www.reserveamerica.com
Open: Year-round
Sites: 119
Amenities: Picnic table, fire ring, water, electricity
Registration: By phone or at park entrance booth
Facilities: Hot showers, flush toilets, pay phone
Fees: $20 per night
Directions: From Port St. Joe, go east on US 98. Go 3 miles and turn right on County Road 30 and follow it 8 miles. Take the sharp right turn on CR 30 East and follow it for 9 miles. It ends where it becomes the park road.

Fort De Soto County Park

Saint Petersburg, Florida

Located just south of the Tampa Bay urban complex, Fort De Soto County Park is a beach camper's getaway located on a chain of small islands dominated by Mullet Key. Pinellas County has done a fantastic job of turning most of this short-lived military base into a getaway for beach lovers.

Fort De Soto features a well-groomed campground with separate areas for tent and RV campers. Nearly three out of every four campsites offer an ocean view. A large staff keeps the park very tidy.

The beaches of Mullet Key have beautiful views of the Tampa Bay area. The beachside accommodations match those views. Recreation opportunities are numerous for De Soto visitors, including beachcombing, canoeing, hiking, biking, and fishing. And the park facilities are very user-friendly. Beach campers will not be disappointed if they come to Fort De Soto County Park. It is the best beach camping anyone could ask for in an urban setting.

The Beach/Coast

The island chain making up the park is at the entrance to Tampa Bay. Madeline Key has the park boat ramp and looks northward toward the mainland. This island and St. Christopher and St. Jean keys are inside the V of Mullet Key in Mullet Key Bayou. Some beach areas are on these keys, but their shoreline is primarily lined with mangroves.

Figure 16. Kayakers take a break at Fort De Soto County Park. Photo by Doug Alderson.

Mullet Key is the largest island in the park. The inner portions of Mullet Key are mangrove areas, forming a harbor of greenery. But the outside of Mullet Key is all beach—more than seven miles of beach line the southern edge of Mullet Key. The East Beach Swim Area is a designated swimming location. Pass more beach. Then come to the Bay Pier, which extends 500 feet into Tampa Bay. Fort De Soto itself is beyond the pier, located at the southern point of Mullet Key, which then turns north. You will immediately come to the 1,000-foot Gulf Pier.

Beyond the Gulf Pier the northward-running beach looks over the Gulf of Mexico and is good for shelling. The shoreline splits and a sandy peninsula is divided by the North Beach Swim Area, a small inlet surrounded by sand and perfect for windy days and children.

The Campground

This campground has three well landscaped and manicured camping areas. Area I is the exclusive domain of tent, van, and pop-up campers. Overhead is a thick forest of live oak and palm growing out of a tangle of palmetto and other brush. Most campsites here have a view into Mullet Key Bayou. Others look over St. Jean Key. In most cases the woods have been cleared to make the most of this view. A larger grassy area parallels a small beach between the campsites and the water. A day room with tables, couches, and a large fireplace offers a potential refuge on inclement days.

Camp Area II, on St. Jean Key, is for RV campers. Again the most is made of the interface between land and sea. All the campsites are in a thick woodland of live oak and palm that is trimmed high, allowing tall motor homes to get in and out of the campsites without damage. One row of campsites backs up to the main park road, but thick vegetation provides an adequate screen. Another row of campsites juts out into Mullet Key Bayou.

Camp Area III, on St. Christopher Key, is also RV only and is the better of the two good RV camping areas. Most campsites have an ocean view. The ones that don't have a view are pull-through sites in the loop center that can accommodate extra-large rigs.

Reservations can now be accepted online. The busy time at Fort De Soto is February through April. Campsites are generally available during the summer except for major holidays, though on summer weekends the park has been known to fill.

Human and Natural History

Fort De Soto, a U.S. installation covering what is now the recreation area, was constructed in 1900. Guns and men were placed in the desolate location. Outbuildings were constructed. Then boredom and misery set in. Biting pests tormented the soldiers. There was simply nothing to do. Lives languished on this lonely key for nine years. Then the place began being manned by an ever more skeletal crew. During World War I, just twenty-six men were left to defend Tampa Bay. By 1923 there was only one soul occupying the whole fort.

The United States government tried to sell the fort but couldn't get a decent bid. For a while the State of Florida had a quarantine station here. Are you getting the idea that this place was thought of as forsaken? To top it all, during World War II Mullet Key was turned into a bombing range! Finally Pinellas County got possession of the island chain and developed it as a park. The design was laid out and the park opened in 1963. In our era of slap-a-condo-everywhere-south-of-Orlando, Mullet Key and the surrounding islands would surely have been developed.

What to Do

Seven miles of beach await you, half facing Tampa Bay, half facing the Gulf of Mexico. This should help you get just the right combination of view, sun, and breeze to suit your fancy. If you want to swim, enjoy the two developed beach areas, East Beach and North Beach. They both have picnic areas, bathroom facilities, and lifeguards in the summer. Some beach areas are posted no swimming. Heed the warnings; there are some wicked currents flowing in and out of Tampa Bay.

Fishermen have all sorts of opportunities. You can surf fish or use one of the two piers—each has a bait and snack shop. Or you can fish Mullet Key Bayou. This needs to be from a self-propelled craft, as most of the bayou is off limits to motorized travel. Canoers and kayakers can enjoy Mullet Key Bayou and a designated canoe trail that winds through the mangroves. A concessionaire rents canoes, kayaks, and nonmotorized vehicles.

A nature trail winds through the habitats of Fort De Soto. Cyclists, roller bladers, and walkers need not use the car, with a 6.8-mile paved recreation trail connecting all the major features of the island. Take a self-guided tour of Fort De Soto. The upper portion of the fort offers a panoramic view of Tampa Bay.

What's Nearby

Most beach campers will find this park fulfilling, but you may get the urge to explore the bay area. Two popular attractions are the Florida Aquarium and Busch Gardens. Busch Gardens is a combination theme park, zoo, museum, and entertainment complex just north of the city of Tampa Bay. The Florida Aquarium replicates the state's many aquatic environments from freshwater springs to coral reefs. Shoreline habitats such as beaches and mangrove forests complete the picture at the aquarium.

Other nearby beaches located along a string of barrier islands extending north from Mullet Key are St. Pete Beach, Treasure Island Beach, and Madeira Beach. All these are also run by Pinellas County.

Information

Fort De Soto County Park
631 Chestnut Street
Clearwater, FL 34616-5336
(813) 866-2662, www.pinellascounty.org
Open: Year-round
Sites: 233
Amenities: Picnic table, standup grill, water, electricity, lantern post
Registration: At park office or by Internet
Facilities: Hot showers, flush toilets, pay phone, laundry
Fees: $25 per night
Directions: From St. Petersburg head south on I-275 to FL 682. Head east on FL 682 to Pinellas Bayway, FL 679. Turn left on Pinellas Bayway and it takes you into Fort De Soto County Park.

Cayo Costa State Park
Boca Grande, Florida

Do you ever dream of escaping to an island where the trappings of civilization are left behind? Then head to Cayo Costa State Park, a barrier island off the southwest Florida coast. It does have some features to enhance your escape. How about a 30-site campground adjacent to a seven-mile stretch of beach? How about some of the best shelling in Florida? How about miles of foot/bicycle trails combing the interior forests of the island?

A trip to Cayo Costa requires a little preplanning. First, arrange your boat shuttle to Cayo Costa from nearby Pine Island. I recommend Tropic Star out of Four Winds Marina on Pine Island. Their number is (239) 283-0015. If you have your own boat, then you are already set. Bring all the food, gear, and supplies that you anticipate needing. The only thing you can purchase on the island is ice, so load your cooler. Get to your ferry on time, hop aboard, and say good-bye to the cruel world as it sinks beyond the horizon.

The Beach/Coast

Cayo Costa is part of the Barrier Islands GEO Park, which includes several islands in the area. Cayo Costa itself is seven miles long and about a mile wide

Figure 17. Wild beach on Cayo Costa. Photo by Doug Alderson.

at its widest point. Your first view of the island is the approach from Pelican Bay as you swing around Punta Blanca Island. Mangrove forms the shoreline, which is punctuated with small inlets and limited narrow beach areas. Other small islands dot the horizon as you look back toward the mainland.

The north tip of Cayo Costa looks over Gasparrilla Island, Boca Grande Pass, and the village of Boca Grande. This is known as Quarantine Point. Then you round the island to the Gulf side. The beach gradually becomes wider. Beyond you is nothing but ocean to the horizon, unless a boat is passing. Here begins the beachcomber's paradise. Small shells pile up along the high tide line. There are no cars or construction noises, just the serenade of the surf. Farther south the island narrows. The beach stretches on for miles; the farther south you walk, the more isolated the beach becomes and the better the shelling becomes.

Arriving at the south tip of the island you look over Captiva Pass at North Captiva Island. Once again, the side facing Pine Island and the mainland becomes dominated by mangrove. Keep heading farther north and you find yourself back at the bayside dock and Pelican Bay.

The Campground

Riding the ferry is just the first step in getting to the campground. Unload your gear off the ferry and register at the campground office. Then load your gear onto the park tram, which takes you about a mile to the Gulf side of the island. The 2004 hurricanes swept through Cayo Costa, leveling the Australian pines and cutting down on shade. Eventually native sea grape and strangler fig trees will provide additional shade for campers.

Several campsites face the beach. These afford little privacy but do have a great ocean view. A second row of campsites is back from the beach. Some of the sites are under a low canopy of vegetation, providing an almost cave-like setting. This row is desirable during times of high wind or cold weather, but it can be buggy. A third row of campsites is integrated into the restored native environment. Some sites are so nestled into the vegetation they are almost hard to find. Bathhouses serve the campground and the adjacent cabins. There are flush toilets and cold outdoor showers. A sink and spigot with potable water are also located at each bathhouse.

Cayo Costa is fairly busy from Thanksgiving until Easter, but you can almost always get a campsite. Reservations can be made, however, eliminating worries. Cayo Costa dies down during the summer months except for the major holidays. Such holidays and during tarpon fishing tournaments are the only times that the campground is guaranteed to be full. Plan accordingly.

Human and Natural History

This island was originally part of the far-flung empire of the Calusa Indians, who occupied many of the barrier islands of the southwest Florida coast. Cuban fishermen, who would stop here to salt and dry their fish before sailing to Cuba, later settled the island. Later yet, the United States saw Cayo Costa as a potential military base to protect the deep Boca Grande Pass, the only entrance to Charlotte harbor. It took thirty-three years to move the settlers; those who had moved to the central part and south end of the island continued their way of life until 1958.

The north end of the island eventually became a county park but in 1983 the state took over the entire operation. Cayo Costa is being restored to its natural state. Park personnel are trying to regrow native species to provide shade as they eliminate the exotic plants. Years from now, Cayo Costa will look very much like all barrier islands did half a millennium ago.

What to Do

While visiting with a fellow camper at Cayo Costa I asked, "What is on your agenda today?" She replied, "That's why I came here—so I wouldn't have an agenda." And that about sums up this place. Cayo Costa is about relaxing, leaving the stresses of work and home behind. It's a vacation, a respite, an escape. It's when you gauge time by the movement of the sun and make your next move when you get the whim. Time to let your mind wander or get lost in that book you've been meaning to read.

And when you are good and ready, there are some popular pastimes at Cayo Costa. Nearly everyone who comes here goes shelling. With no auto access, there are more shells for those who make the effort to get here. Here's a tip for shellers: the farther south you head from the campground, the more interesting the shells you are apt to find. Or perhaps you'd just like to walk the beach and listen to the waves and watch the birds and feel the wind blow through your hair.

Hikers and those who bring bikes can enjoy the many miles of trails that crisscross the island. You can see an old island cemetery or get a view from

Quarantine Point or hike along the Gulf. I had a ball biking around the island. Be apprised that mosquitoes can be troublesome in the island's interior.

What's Nearby

Since Cayo Costa is a barrier island with no road access, your options outside the park are limited. However, some of the ferry services take visitors to nearby Cabbage Key, which is visible from the bay side dock and has a restaurant and bar. This is reputedly the restaurant where Jimmy Buffet, then an unknown singer, was inspired to write the song "Cheeseburger in Paradise." Beyond Cabbage Key, it is up to you to make your own paradise on Cayo Costa.

Information

Barrier Islands GEO Park
P.O. Box 1150
Boca Grande, FL 33921
(941) 964-0375, www.floridastateparks.org; camping reservations (800) 326-3521, www.reserveamerica.com; Tropic Star ferry reservations (239) 283-0015
Open: Year-round
Sites: 30
Amenities: Picnic table, fire ring
Registration: First come, first serve only
Facilities: Cold showers, flush toilets, water spigot
Fees: $18 per night
Directions: From North Fort Myers take FL 78 for 16 miles to Pine Island. Turn right where FL 78 ends and go 4 miles to Four Winds Marina. It will be on your left. The Tropic Star will boat you out to Cayo Costa.

Flamingo Campground

Flamingo, Florida

Flamingo campground is located on the most southerly part of the U.S. mainland. Farther south are island-studded Florida Bay and the Florida Keys. To the north is the largest roadless area in the lower forty-eight states: the Everglades. Flamingo Campground is headquarters for all those who wish to explore one of America's finest natural resources, Everglades National Park.

From your headquarters you can see what the Everglades are really all about: a vast ecosystem powered by water that moves from the plains of sawgrass through the richest stands of mangrove on the planet to pristine undeveloped beaches astride the Gulf and then to scores of remote ocean islands, all protected by national park status. And between the park service and a concessionaire, you'll never have to leave the former fishing village before at least a portion of your curiosity has been sated. Once the spell of the 'Glades has been cast, most likely you'll be back for more.

The Beach/Coast

Everglades National Park covers far more coastline than any other park in this book. Starting just south of the Miami metroplex, the park encompasses the

Figure 18. Campers serenade the wind on the edge of Florida Bay at Flamingo Campground.

small islands of Florida Bay and the mangrove shorelines east of Flamingo, where crocodiles thrive. Closer to Flamingo are points of land that jut into Florida Bay, and a coastal prairie provides vistas of the waters and islands of the bay.

Flamingo has a full-scale marina where boats of all sizes and descriptions come and go. Then begins Cape Sable, which I describe as "one of the finest pieces of real estate in North America." A series of beaches stretches first west and then north, encompassing the southwest tip of Florida. The Coastal Prairie Trail extends along the southerly tip of the cape. Backcountry campsites for boaters occupy selected points along the cape.

North of Cape Sable begin alternating stretches of beach and mangrove coastline accessible only by boat. Highland Beach rises right from the ocean. Be apprised that no beaches can be accessed by land; however, you can access Florida Bay directly from much of the campground.

The famous Ten Thousand Islands begin north of Highland Beach. Here a myriad of small mangrove islands form a coastal maze that extends miles up the coast beyond Everglades City. Some keys have small beaches; all exude a sense of wild remoteness seldom seen on the American coast.

The Campground

Flamingo Campground, located directly on Florida Bay, is laid back and moves with the pace of the sun moving across the sky, like a former fishing village should. The campground has a walk-in tent area, a mixed area, and a trailer area. The camping area with auto pull-ins consists of four loops. Each loop is an oval with side roads cutting across it, like rows in movie theater. Each of these side roads has from five to ten campsites, which lie beneath landscaped native trees such as buttonwood, gumbo-limbo, and palm. These tropical trees add to the seaside atmosphere. Each loop has a bathhouse. There are no water or electrical hookups. You must get your water from spigots by the bathhouses.

The tent camping area, with 64 campsites, is situated in a grassy field with a few palm trees, overlooking Florida Bay. There is far more sun than shade. You tote your gear a short distance to your tent site from a common parking area. The setting is scenic, but the lack of shade can be bothersome on a hot day. The openness of the campground is a plus with respect to insects, however, since breezes sweep through unfettered.

The bugs and heat all but shut the campground down by May after a season beginning in November. The winter months can be fantastic, with warm days and cool nights. Reservations are rarely necessary with nearly 300 campsites, but you may wish to call ahead for peace of mind. The busy times are between Christmas and New Year's Day, Martin Luther King Day, and the Presidents' Day weekend.

Human and Natural History

The whole system of the Everglades is based on the seasonal flow of water, and the alteration of that flow changes everything. From the Kissimmee River Basin to the north, fresh water moves southward through the sawgrass in a thin sheet several miles wide. In this sawgrass are islands of higher ground, where tropical trees grow in "hammocks," forming small ecosystems of their own where deer and the reclusive panther reside.

As the fresh water spreads south, it meets the salt water of the ocean, melding with the ebb and flow of the tides. Here mangrove stands rise from the rich waters. Dolphins and sharks swim alongside gamefish. Smaller fish are fare for the incredible variety of birds, including ospreys and herons.

Finally, the now brackish water enters the Gulf of Mexico, Florida Bay, and the Ten Thousand Islands. The only place the crocodile occurs in the United States is in the southeastern Everglades. The only place in the world where the alligator and crocodile reside side by side is in the Everglades. But this is just one distinctive aspect of the unique ecosystem that is the Everglades.

What to Do

The southern side of the park harbors many different environments. On your way in, make your first stop the Coe Visitor Center. The museum and displays explain the web of life making up the Everglades. Beyond the visitor center are the Pinelands. Hikers can enjoy the miles of trails that course through pine forest in some of the driest land in the 'Glades. Get a view from Pa-hay-okee Overlook. Stop at Mahogany Hammock and make a loop on the elevated boardwalk through a tropical hardwood hammock. Next, head to Flamingo and set up camp. Catch a South Florida sunset, then plan your activities for the next day.

You can use your feet, a canoe, motorboat, sailboat, tour boat, or automobile to explore the landscape. A park-authorized concessionaire has rentals if you don't bring your own craft. Eco Pond, a walking destination, is popular with birders. A quiet canoe trip sometimes reaps large rewards for ecotourists. The Nine Mile Pond Canoe Trail actually travels only five miles. Since motors are not allowed, you quickly get back to communing with the real world—the natural world. Fishermen can work a pole into watery plans for outings everywhere from small creeks to big Florida Bay.

Or you can take a cruise into the backcountry, Florida Bay, or Whitewater Bay—or sail into the sunset. Contact the concessionaire for departures and prices of sightseeing cruises. There is more here to do than most campers have time to squeeze in.

What's Nearby

The Flamingo experience at Everglades National Park is an all-inclusive endeavor. There is plenty to see and do in this vast preserve. Before you enter the park, round up all the supplies you think you will need. There is a marina store, but it charges high prices for limited supplies. Try to keep your purchases to ice and souvenirs and you'll be fine.

Information

Everglades National Park
40001 State Road
Homestead, FL 33034
(305) 242-7700; www.nps.gov/ever; camping reservations (800) 365-2267, www.reservations.nps.gov
Open: Year-round
Sites: 288
Amenities: Picnic table, standup grill; some sites have fire rings
Registration: By phone or at park entrance booth
Facilities: Water spigot, cold showers, flush toilets, pay phone
Fees: $14 per night
Directions: From US 1 in Florida City, follow the signs south to Everglades National Park. Flamingo Campground is 38 miles beyond the Everglades entrance gate on Main Park Road.

Bahia Honda State Park
Big Pine Key, Florida

It's the beaches. The beaches are the number one attraction at Bahia Honda State Park. For all their extended coastline, the Keys have surprisingly few beaches, so these beaches and their alluring waters are a strong draw. Bahia Honda's Sandspur Beach has in the past been voted the best in America.

Not surprisingly, most other activities are oriented toward the water. The inviting aquamarine sea, punctuated by darker patches of sea grass, offers fishing, boating, snorkeling, kayaking, and every other mode of movement over water, including parasailing.

Being so attractive draws a crowd. Bahia Honda is positively hopping. Smart campers make reservations. The three park campgrounds all offer different views of this 524-acre park. When you arrive, relax, take your time, and enjoy the park. Be sure to schedule a day to visit Key West to glimpse this quirky coastal island town with its eclectic flair.

The Beach/Coast

Tropical flora and stunningly colorful and clear water lapping at the sand combine to make some great beach at Bahia Honda. Three beaches offer wa-

Figure 19. This is but one of the beaches at glorious Bahia Honda State Park.

terside variety at the park. Calusa Beach looks out on the Bahia Honda rail-road bridge and a continuous stretch of scenic shoreline. Picnic shelters and palm trees border the roped-off swimming area. The calm waters are ideal for young children. Next up the coast is Loggerhead Beach. Four walkways lead down from the elevated old US 1 down to the sand. This beach is continuous and enters a small cove broken up by a tidal creek. Past the cove is a stretch of exposed Key Largo limestone, the foundation of the island.

Then comes the park's best beach, Sandspur Beach. Two picnic shelters flank a central bathhouse. The beach is wide, especially by Keys standards. The waters are often calm and nearly always clear. Boaters are seen out on the horizon. Nearby, beachgoers are engaged in a variety of pursuits, including doing absolutely nothing. Sandspur Beach extends to the channel between Bahia Honda and Ohio Key. This channel is lined with mangrove, as is the north side of Bahia Honda, though there are rocky areas of exposed lime-stone. Then you come to the deep dredged inlet near the park cabins and Bay Side Camping Area and finally to US 1.

The Campground

Each of the three camping areas at Bahia Honda exudes a different ambiance. The 48-site Buttonwood Camping Area, all sites with water and electricity, is the sole campground RVs can use. Vegetation featuring palms and sea grape divides the campsites, but it is low slung and offers little shade overhead. Some campsites have an ocean view and breezes. There are some slips for campers' boats here. But these campsites also face out to noisy US 1.

You reach the Bay Side Camping Area after passing under the low clear-ance of US 1. It has eight sites in a row along an old dredged inlet. These eight sites, with water only, are for tents, vans, and pop-ups that can go below the 6-foot, 8-inch clearance of US 1. Set apart from the others and near Sandspur Beach is the Sandspur Camping Area. Its 24 campsites are literally cut out of a dense tropical forest. The first eight sites have water only and are away from the ocean in the darkest woods. The next 16 campsites all have both water and electricity. Eleven of them are oceanside. You get a combination of shade and ocean access and perhaps some breezes. The thick hammock dulls the sounds of US 1.

This campground is busy nearly all the time. From November through August the campground is full every night. A few summer weeknights see some vacancies. Fall is the least busy time here, but don't take chances. Make your reservations as far in advance as possible.

Human and Natural History

Just a few miles southwest of Bahia Honda is Big Pine Key, primary habitat of one of the rarest, most threatened, and cutest animals in the United States, the Key deer. These small deer, a subspecies of the Virginia whitetail, stand only two to three feet high at the shoulder. Back in the 1940s their very existence was in peril. Less than forty animals were known to exist. In 1957, the National Key Deer Refuge was established, and the population has stabilized at around three hundred animals. Most of these are on Big Pine Key and No Name Key, but they range from Johnson Keys in the east to Sugarloaf Keys in the west.

The deer are believed to have migrated this way when the Keys were a continuous land bridge during the latter ice ages. Then, as the ice melted, the sea rose, forming the Keys and limiting the range of the deer. Indians, Spaniards, and wreck salvagers used the deer as a food source. Uncontrolled hunting and loss of habitat brought the deer to the brink of extinction before the establishment of the refuge. You can visit the National Key Deer Refuge on Big Pine Key. It is located just off US 1 on Key Deer Boulevard.

What to Do

With three beaches in the park, your main task is to find the one you like. There is plenty of beachfront and even more waterfront. Pure relaxation and escape from the rat race are the main adult diversions. Building sand castles works for kids. Some folks favor fishing. Snorkeling is rewarding in the clear water; snorkeling tours are led daily. Sea kayaks are another popular way to get on the ocean. If you want to get on the water and let someone else handle the steering, take a boat tour. The park concessionaire offers this and rents out just about everything else you might need at Bahia Honda: pontoon boats, fishing boats, one- and two-person kayaks, fishing rods, and bicycles.

What's Nearby

Many campers use Bahia Honda as a base to explore Key West. This island at the end of Florida is one of the state's most historic, occupied from the days of the Calusa Indians and the Spaniards to construction of Fort Zachary Taylor and a setting for wreck salvagers and Ernest Hemmingway. Take the Conch Train and tour Old Town and Duval Street. Climb the Key West

Lighthouse and enjoy the view of the town. The Key West Shipwreck Histo-reum will inform you about boats that have foundered in the shifting shoals of the southernmost United States. Of course, watching the sun go down at Key West has become a spectator sport.

Information

Bahia Honda State Park
36850 Overseas Highway
Big Pine Key, FL 33043
(305) 872-2353, www.floridastateparks.org, www.bahiahondapark.com; camp-ing reservations (800) 326-3521, www.reserveamerica.com
Open: Year-round
Sites: 66 water and electricity, 16 water only
Amenities: Picnic table, grill, water spigot; all but 8 sites have electricity
Registration: By phone or at park entrance booth
Facilities: Hot showers, flush toilets
Fees: $26 per night
Directions: Bahia Honda State Park is on the east side of US 1 at mile marker 36.5.

Long Key State Recreation Area
Layton, Florida

You'll have a hard time finding a campground with more crystal-clear, sky-blue water around it than at Long Key. Set in the center of the Florida Keys with the Atlantic Ocean on one side and Florida Bay on the other, this state recreation area not only has an oceanside campground but is also a Mecca for water sports. The Middle Keys are often called the sport fishing capital of the world, but the most beautiful water in the state might keep you from focusing on your rod. That exquisite aquamarine water is also why boating, canoeing, and studying marine ecology draw people here. So does simply looking over the Atlantic from your campsite.

Why wouldn't the water be a draw? From the mainland to Key West there is far more ocean than land. The resources of the sea have drawn people here for thousands of years, creating an interesting history that you can learn about while here at Long Key. Nearby are two-state owned islands, Lignumvitae Key and Indian Key, where the history of the Keys is showcased.

The Beach/Coast

Considering the amount of water around, there is far less classic beach at Long Key than one would imagine. In most of the Keys the tropical forest

Figure 20. Long Key State Park at low tide.

Figure 21. Long Key State Park canoe dock. Photo by Doug Alderson.

and mangrove grow right to the water's edge, with minimal sandy transition areas before the stunning sea. But don't let that stop you; there are sandy spots large enough to lay your body down—just not large enough to throw your Frisbee.

The north side of Long Key, which faces Florida Bay, is exposed rocky coral reef leading right to the water. In other areas mangrove forms the transition area between land and sea. As you move south around Long Key Point the mangrove gives way to a narrow strip of beach looking out over the Atlantic Ocean. The warm Gulf Stream, the current where so many ships travel, is just a few miles out to sea. The reefs of the Keys lie perilously close to the Gulf Stream, which has resulted in many ships wrecking offshore, and this in turn has led to the wrecking business becoming an important part of Keys history.

The most popular swimming location is beyond the shaded picnic area. Here, rocks line the island to prevent erosion. A small pier has steps that lead right to the ocean. Farther down begins the campground, flanked by a narrow beach backing up against a small dune running parallel to the ocean. Swimmers can be found here too. Here and there grows a stray mangrove. This narrow beach extends beyond the campground to the end of the park.

The Campground

This campground has views among the best in Florida. Every one of the 60 campsites overlooks the Atlantic Ocean. The water offshore is aquamarine with darker patches of blue off in the distance. The campground is laid out along one slender paved road. This section of Long Key is narrow, but the Keys are land-poor to start with, so the drone of US 1 is hard to escape anywhere down here. Let it be known that road noise is a drawback to this campground.

The campsites are generally narrow, though an average RV can fit into almost any site. Tropical trees such poisonwood, buttonwood, and gumbo-limbo adorn the campground. Between the ocean and each campsite is a small wooden barrier to protect the dunes, sea oats, and other shoreline plants; a small path leads from each site to the seaside. Large elevated bathhouses are evenly spaced along the campground road.

The park also has seven primitive campsites bordering the Atlantic. Mangrove blocks the ocean view. Campers have to carry gear from the car to the campsites along a wooden walkway. Each wooden platform site is shaded by a roof and served by an outdoor cold shower and water spigot. The lack of breeze, presence of insects, and distance from car to campsite means these sites are mainly used by younger, hardier campers who appreciate the low price.

Long Key is at its busiest from mid-December to mid-March. It is a rare day that every campsite is not occupied during this time. Don't waste your time driving down here and taking your chances. Make a reservation. Summer is busy, too.

Human and Natural History

The Gulf Stream flows very near Long Key. Its closeness to the shallow water of the Keys has inevitably led to wrecks. Key West became an important wreck salvaging center. Then one Jacob Houseman established his own wrecking center on Indian Key, a few miles northeast of Long Key. His success made the competition at Key West angry, especially when he got the state to form Dade County with Indian Key as the county seat. The Key Westers of Monroe County took him to court and finally drove him out of business.

Long Key remained remote until Henry Flagler extended the Florida East

Coast Railroad to Key West in the early 1900s. Long Key entered its golden age. With author Zane Grey at the helm, the Long Key Fishing Club established a plush fishing resort here. Famous anglers from around the world fished these waters and established a policy of protecting many of the game-fish they sought. However, a hurricane wiped out the railroad and fishing club in 1935, also destroying a coconut plantation that was on the site of Long Key State Recreation Area. Later US 1 was built on fill and pilings from the old railroad, establishing the auto access from the mainland to the Keys that we see today.

What to Do

Long Key is geared toward water-oriented activities. You can simply step forth from your campsite and take a dip in the beautiful waters of the Atlantic. Swimming and snorkeling are a delight in these clear waters. Fishermen wade beyond the campsites, trying to nail bonefish. You can fish from a canoe in the Atlantic or Florida Bay or head south a short way on US 1 and angle from the old bridge between Long Key and Conch Key.

If you want to plunk down some money you can rent a boat, take a charter, or get on a group boat. Or you can take a tour boat out to Lignumvitae Key or Indian Key. Ranger-led tours show people around the historic islands to explore the human and natural history of these keys. Long Key park personnel have the pertinent information.

Back at Long Key, trail lovers can walk the Golden Orb Trail, which pierces the mangrove and makes a loop. The Layton Trail enters a dark tropical hammock and identifies the unusual fauna of Long Key. Bicyclists can pedal park roads out to US 1 and follow a paved path that leads in either direction.

What's Nearby

North of you is Islamorada, "the Purple Isle." This is where Lignumvitae Key and Indian Key are. South of you is Marathon, the heart of the Keys and the nearest location for a full-service grocery store and other major supplies. There is a convenience store just north of the park.

Another swimming area is Annes Beach, a county property on US 1 about 10 miles to the north, where the beach is wider than that at Long Key.

Information

Long Key State Recreation Area
US 1, P.O. Box 776
Long Key, FL 33001
(305) 664-4815, www.floridastateparks.org; reservations (800) 326-3521, www.reserveamerica.com

Open: Year-round

Sites: 60 full facility sites, 7 primitive sites

Amenities: Full facility sites have picnic table, fire ring, water, electricity; primitive sites have picnic table, upright grill, shelter roof

Registration: By phone or at park entrance booth

Facilities: Hot showers, flush toilets

Fees: Full facility sites $26 per night, primitive sites $7 per night

Directions: Long Key State Recreation Area is at mile marker 67.5 on US 1.

John Pennekamp Coral Reef State Park
Key Largo, Florida

This state park holds the distinction of being the America's first undersea park. However, before you imagine an underwater campground, understand that some above-ground shoreline goes along with the 178 nautical miles of coral reefs and other ocean environments beneath clear warm waters ideal for snorkeling and scuba diving.

This busy park has a passable campground to go along with multiple facilities to further your enjoyment of the reefs. Concessionaires operate glass-bottomed boats, snorkeling, sailing, and diving operations inside the park. Above-water attractions include two beaches, two hiking trails, and a 30,000-gallon aquarium at the visitor center.

Just about everyone gets in or on the water one way or another. Many fishermen and divers embark from the park's marina; others canoe and kayak. Still others rent sea cycles, bumper boats, and small sailboats. This is an active

Figure 22. The author looks out over the water off John Pennekamp.

camper's park; nearly everyone is busy doing something. So if you have come to watch the breeze blow, look out—someone is likely to knock you down on the way to that clear water to see the living coral reef.

The Beach/Coast

The land portion of John Pennekamp is situated on Key Largo, at the southwestern edge of Largo Sound. Largo Sound forms a bay between Key Largo and Radabob Key, a mangrove island that lies between the state park and the Atlantic Ocean. Two channels lead north and south out of Largo Sound to the Atlantic. Fascinating undersea life thrives in Largo Sound and beyond into the Atlantic.

In the developed area of John Pennekamp the mangrove gives way first to Cannon Beach, a popular swimming and snorkeling area. Here palm and sea grape trees form some seaside shade near actual mounted cannons on the sand. The sand leads down to a roped-off swimming area with a floating pier, and a replica of a Spanish shipwreck lies in the translucent blue water.

Beyond Cannon Beach is the main marina area, where you can embark on many watery pursuits. A boat ramp and slips for private boats are located here. Across the bridge from the marina is a mangrove and sand island with another swimming area. Swimmers and snorkelers interact with the water and the life within it.

Also on this island is a boardwalk that cuts through a mangrove thicket and follows a tidal creek. At the end of the walkway is Far Beach, the most popular beach for sunbathers. A shaded picnic shelter and palm trees stand next to a clear pool of ocean water. A circular rock partition divides the swimming area from the rest of Largo Sound. Other small creeks and channels wind through the mangroves nearby.

The Campground

The campground doesn't begin to match the underwater or other aboveground facilities at John Pennekamp. It is the weak link among the park's developed areas. This is not to say don't camp here; just don't make camping here an end in itself. Camp here as a means of enjoying the other recreational opportunities at John Pennekamp.

The campground lies along a wide two-way gravel road that spurs off the marina parking lot. The campsites flank the road's C-shaped curve, with a tidal creek on one side and a mangrove thicket on the other. A floor of gravel over hard rock makes it challenging to stake your tent. Twenty-two of the 47 campsites back up to the tidal creek. A decent cover of buttonwood, palm, gumbo-limbo, and sea grape shades the first few campsites, along with some mangrove, which grows on the edge of the tidal creek.

Despite being one of the least appealing of Florida's coastal campgrounds, John Pennekamp stays very busy. It is full virtually every night from December through the winter and beyond into the summer. The threat of hurricanes is the only thing that keeps campers away from here. Make a reservation months in advance if you want to park your rig or pitch your tent at John Pennekamp.

Human and Natural History

Miami newspaperman John D. Pennekamp realized that private and commercial divers were harvesting the fragile resources of this undersea wonderland, the only living coral reef system off the U.S. mainland. The coral reefs of John Pennekamp are ocean habitats that provide a foundation for many marine plants and animals. Corals are themselves alive, being made up of tiny animals known as polyps. The limestone skeleton of a reef forms from polyp secretions, and succeeding generations of new polyps growing on the outer sections of the structure are what make it a living coral reef. Around the reefs are other kinds of living corals and a host of undersea creatures like the spiny lobster, turtles, and lots of fish.

Another important community of the greater Keys Marine Sanctuary is the sea grass meadows. Sea grasses are among the few flowering plants that grow entirely under the water. Sea grass cleanses water and stabilizes the floor of shallow tidal areas while providing a food source for manatees and supplying sheltered, nutrient-rich habitat for turtles, shrimp, and smaller fish; the many tiny inhabitants of sea grass meadows in turn attract larger fish and birds. Mangroves act as a filter to trap land debris and to provide habitat for small fish that are a key part of the food chain. Together, the three communities of coral reefs, mangroves, and sea grass meadows all work to keep the ocean clean and to support the riot of undersea life around the Keys.

What to Do

First, head to the park visitor center and see the 30,000-gallon aquarium, where you can view a reef environment in comfort. The spiny lobsters and tropical fish are quite a sight. Now you are primed for the real thing. All the equipment and instruction needed to explore the reefs are onsite at John Pennekamp. If you aren't in the mood to get wet, take the glass-bottomed boat tour. This two-and-a-half-hour trip passes over some interesting life forms beneath the clear waters.

Snorkeling is easy to learn and doesn't require certification, as diving does. If you don't feel comfortable renting your gear and hitting the water on your own, join a snorkeling tour and learn with other greenhorns. You can also double your fun by heading to sea on a catamaran and sailing to a good snorkeling location. If snorkeling makes you want to go deeper, you can learn to dive here from certified instructors. Experienced divers can get openwater or advanced openwater certification. Anglers can enjoy this water too, getting only a line wet, fishing for a variety of saltwater species.

Two short nature trails familiarize visitors with the flora of the area. The Tamarind Trail explores a tropical hardwood hammock, while the Mangrove Trail follows a boardwalk through a shoreline mangrove thicket. Or you can view the mangrove from the water by canoe or kayak on a 2.5-mile marked paddling trail. Should you need a few hours of relaxation after exploring America's first undersea park, Cannon Beach and Far Beach await you.

What's Nearby

The coral reefs are the primary attraction of Key Largo and environs. But just to the northwest of Key Largo is the vastness of Everglades National Park, where there is a world of nature to explore. Newspaperman John Pennekamp was also instrumental in the establishment of the Everglades park. Ten miles south of John Pennekamp is the Florida Keys Wild Bird Rehabilitation Center. Injured birds are nursed here for release back into the wild. You can see these birds as they recover. The *African Queen*, the boat made famous by the movie of the same name starring Humphrey Bogart and Katherine Hepburn, is on display nearby.

Information

John Pennekamp Coral Reef State Park
P.O. Box 487
Key Largo, FL 33037
(305) 451-1202, www.floridastateparks.org, www.johnpennekamp.com; reservations (800) 326-3521, www.reserveamerica.com
Open: Year-round
Sites: 47
Amenities: Picnic table, fire ring, water, electricity
Registration: By phone or at park entrance booth
Facilities: Hot showers, flush toilets, pay phone
Fees: $26 per night
Directions: John Pennekamp Coral Reef State Park is south of Miami at mile marker 102.5 off US 1 on Key Largo. The park is on your left.

Sebastian Inlet State Recreation Area

Melbourne Beach, Florida

This region of Florida is known as the Treasure Coast. It was named after the offshore sinking of a Spanish fleet laden with gold and gems from Mexico, South America, and the Orient. Today Sebastian Inlet is a natural gem among the gold and jewels that lie hidden beneath the Atlantic waves.

A magnet for water sports, specifically fishing and surfing, Sebastian Inlet has been developed with ocean lovers in mind. More than four miles of beach face the strong Atlantic waves, where surfers try to "hang ten." The waves here are among the best on the entire East Coast. Other park visitors indulge in less strenuous pursuits, like watching the surfers. Jetties, piers, a bait store, and marina make the park convenient for fishing.

Ecotourism is on the rise here also, with the proximity of Pelican Island, America's oldest wildlife refuge, and the Archie Carr National Wildlife Refuge. Much of the park also abuts the Indian River Lagoon, North America's most diverse estuary.

The Beach/Coast

Since this park is located on Orchid Island, a barrier island, nearly the entire park is surrounded by coastline. Sebastian Inlet itself is a manmade cut, re-

Figure 23. Sebastian Inlet is popular with surfers and pier fishermen.

dredged in 1947; the original cut connecting the Indian River with the Atlantic was made in 1918. The park is divided into two sections. Starting in the north, two miles from the inlet, the Atlantic beach rises fairly sharply from the blue waters. Usually a level bench of sand marks the high tide line. Behind the tan sand is a low-slung maritime forest. The lovely stretch of beach continues to the inlet, where two jetties banked with rocks protect the inlet from filling in. This picture-perfect Florida beach continues south of the inlet, offering ample space for everyone.

The west side of the barrier island is primarily mangrove bordering the rich Indian River Lagoon, which has an average depth of three feet. The mangrove shoreline twists and turns, overlooking smaller mangrove islands, then returns north to the inlet again. In times of strong tides, water rushes through the pass with considerable force. North of the inlet the mangrove resumes its winding form and eventually comes to Inlet Marina, run by a state park concessionaire.

The Campground

The campground is located on a small peninsula between Sebastian Inlet and a small tidal lagoon of Indian River. This setup makes for some decent bug-ridding ocean breezes. The campground is hilly by Florida standards, since it is built on dredge spoil from the dredging of Sebastian Inlet. Sea grape, gumbo-limbo, cabbage palm, and cedar provide cover.

Three rows of campsites are situated along two loops. As you enter the campground, the first loop has 14 sites on a small elongated knoll overlooking the Indian River. These campsites are the least vegetated and the smallest, yet people manage to park RV rigs and still have room for folding chairs and the like.

The second row of campsites is in the middle of the campground. In addition to native trees, brush such as privet and salt myrtle separates the campsites, which are medium to small in size. Moving southward, a large area of native vegetation is growing up around two bathhouses, each with hot showers, flush toilets, laundry, and a phone. A third row of campsites lies next to a thick growth of mangrove bordering a tidal lagoon. These 16 campsites are on natural ground and are low lying compared to the rest of the campground. Divided by planted natural vegetation, these sites are the largest, with adequate room for any RV or the largest tent-camping family. The price you pay to get into one of these sites is the absence of a view.

Sebastian Inlet is enjoying increased popularity and is busier than ever. Generally, the campsite composition is 7 to 1 RVs to tents during winter. More tenters come in the summer. The campground is full of snowbirds between December and mid-April. Summer weekends and holidays fill too. Get reservations during these periods.

Human and Natural History

When Spain was a world power the Spaniards plundered the seas for riches to render them even more powerful. After gathering treasures from the New World, ships would meet in Cuba to sail en masse back to Spain. The long journey, which passed northward along the Florida coast, was always dangerous, but no amount of armament could help sailors defy a hurricane that sank the entire fleet of ships that fateful August of 1715. More than a thousand men washed up on the land, only to face the glaring sun and relentless insects. They feared the Indians, too. But the Ais Indians actually gave them food. Yet many sailors died waiting for the wreck salvagers from Havana. The salvagers recovered only half of the loot. The rest lay at the bottom of the sea, washed over by the shifting sands beneath the waves.

In the 1950s another hurricane struck, altering the coastline and exposing the salvagers' camp. Next, a fellow named Kip Wagner found one of the ships, and treasure hunters donning scuba gear hit the mother lode—gold bars, doubloons, and jewelry as well as more archaeologically significant artifacts that are a window into the everyday world of the Spanish sailor. These artifacts are on display at the recreation area's McLarty Museum, underscoring why the region is called the Treasure Coast.

What to Do

Surfers take on the waves year-round. Surfing is not on the menu for most of us, but even if you don't surf, walk out on the north jetty and watch the brave souls riding the waves, sometimes going a long way, sometimes crashing in an eruption of white foam.

There are so many places to fish here, and an onsite tackle and bait shop makes fishing even easier. The prime angling spots are from one of the two jetties along the inlet. Below the bridge that spans Sebastian Inlet are two catwalks extending over the inlet. Other fishermen favor surf fishing, and yet others try their luck in the Indian River Lagoon. For those with a boat the options include ranging farther out in the lagoon and out to the sea. You can rent canoes, kayaks, and motorboats at the park marina to tool around Indian River Lagoon and explore the wildlife refuge. Take the ranger-led cruise aboard the *Inlet Explorer* and see what birds and sea creatures turn up in the lagoon.

With over four miles of beach right on the Atlantic, you can walk the tan sand till your feet shrivel. But if you lie still, don't be surprised to find yourself lulled into a nap by the crashing waves. If you get tired of walking the sand, take the park nature trail and learn about the maritime forest of this protected barrier island.

What's Nearby

North of the Treasure Coast is what's known as the Space Coast, the Cape Canaveral area. Here you can go to the astronaut hall of fame and enjoy other celestial pursuits. Nature lovers have the Cape Canaveral National Seashore to enjoy. It has miles and miles of beach and tidal areas to explore. Camping is limited to primitive backcountry only.

Information

Sebastian Inlet State Recreation Area
9700 South US A1A
Melbourne Beach, FL 32951
(321) 984-4852, www.floridastateparks.org; reservations (800) 326-3521, www.reserveamerica.com
Open: year-round
Sites: 51
Amenities: Picnic table, fire ring, water, electricity
Registration: By phone or at park entrance booth
Facilities: Hot showers, flush toilets, pay phone, laundry
Fees: $23 per night
Directions: From Vero Beach head east on FL 60 to US A1A. Turn left on US A1A and head north on it for about 10 miles to Sebastian Inlet State Recreation Area.

Gamble Rogers Memorial State Recreation Area
Flagler Beach, Florida

Beachfront camping is the major attraction here, and this is the last Atlantic beachfront camping between the town of Flagler Beach and the Keys to the south. Located just south of town, this small recreation area of only 144 acres packs a powerful punch. The Atlantic sweeps right up to the reddish tan sands, which rise to a wind-sculpted grassy dune that is more like a bluff. Atop this bluff sits the campground. Across US A1A is the rest of the park.

Use Gamble Rogers as a base camp to explore the other beaches of the area as well as the cultural and historic sights of this quiet section of Atlantic coastline. Nearby are county and state beaches, including one of the state's newer acquisitions, North Peninsula State Recreation Area. Farther inland are Bulow Creek State Park, home of the ancient Fairchild Oak, and the Bulow Plantation Ruins State Historic Site, where you can see relics of an old sugar mill and gain insight into life on a sugar plantation of the early 1800s.

Figure 24. The beach at Gamble Rogers Memorial State Recreation Area is formed from coquina rock.

The Beach/Coast

Gamble Rogers is limited in size and has only about a quarter mile of Atlantic coastline. The colorful orange sands are made of shell crushed by pounding from the waves. When compacted, such shell forms a rock known as coquina, which means "little shell" in Spanish. The high bluff along this coast lies atop the coquina rock.

Only about 100 feet of beach separate the Atlantic from the salt-spray-pruned grass and palmetto-covered dunes that rise steeply, then level off on top of the coquina, which is also covered in low-lying dune vegetation. Being below this bluff makes you feel almost closed in with the Atlantic.

Two boardwalks lead down from the day use parking area to the beach. There is an outdoor shower and an indoor bathhouse for day users. Moving southward along the beach you come to five more boardwalks connecting the beach to the campground. Such direct beach access from the campground is the big drawing card for Gamble Rogers.

There are several other beach areas to enjoy nearby. Just a few miles south is the North Peninsula State Recreation Area, with its uninterrupted 2.5-mile stretch of beach. Beachcombers can stretch a leg and watch the coast meld away in the distance. North of Gamble Rogers is the actual Flagler Beach and the city pier, where many people fish. Farther north is Beverly Beach and the rocky coastline at Washington Oaks State Gardens.

The Campground

You are one with the ocean at this intimate campground, with only 34 campsites sandwiched between the Atlantic and US A1A. On a windy or stormy day the waves seem as if they will come over the bluff and wash out the campground. However, the drop from the campground down to the water is a good 30 or 40 feet. Overhead, there is little vegetation, save for a few palm trees. The rest of the vegetation is salt-pruned grasses and palmetto. Ocean breezes waft right through, which keeps the insects down in the warmer months but also keeps a chill on when the weather is cool.

Passing the campground gate you come to a boardwalk leading to the ocean after campsite #5 and another after campsite #11. The vegetation falls away on the seaward side, revealing a nice ocean view. Ten more campsites are beyond the bathhouse. You have glimpses of US A1A, complete views of your neighbors, and wide open ocean vistas. The openness of the campground discourages many tent campers from coming here. It is generally windier here in the winter, so tent campers are better off in the summer. RV campers find the large sites much to their liking: one can park a rig and still have plenty of room to set out the lawn chairs, and when the wind blows RVers can simply escape the elements inside the rig.

Gamble Rogers is a popular year-round recreation destination. Once March rolls around you can expect a full house every night until September. Make reservations at these times of year. Things calm down in early fall, then the cold weather sends the snowbirds south from December on, though weeknights offer a few open campsites.

Human and Natural History

The Bulow Plantation State Historic Site contains the remnants of an old sugar mill that is well worth your time to tour. In the 1820s Charles Bulow cleared 2,200 acres of land along the creek that now bears his name, planting sugar cane, among other crops. The cane was processed into sugar at the plantation. You can walk the remains of the sugar mill today.

The woods here were once fields where cane was cut to be brought to the mill and placed on a conveyor. A boiler-powered engine operated rollers that crushed the cane, the juice falling into settling vats. The leftover cane fiber, called bagasse, was hauled away. The cane juice flowed from vats on the top floor into a series of five kettles. Then the juice was hand dipped from larger to smaller kettles and ended up as syrup.

When the syrup reached the "strike" stage, it was turning to sugar. The syrup was placed in large wooden cooling vats to harden. Then the solid product was cut up and placed into wooden barrels. The barrels were loaded onto wagons and hauled to a boat landing, where the sugar was shipped off to St. Augustine or Jacksonville.

What to Do

As indicated, being able to walk directly from your campsite to the ocean is one of the best things about Gamble Rogers. This offers a fine opportunity for watching Atlantic sunrises. Many people just plop right down on a beach chair as the sun makes its way across the sky, perhaps getting into the water a time or two to cool off. This place is all about relaxation. If you want to beachcomb, go down to the North Peninsula Recreation Area. Beachcombers may also want to head north to see the gardens and rocky shoreline of Washington Oaks.

Surf fishermen can set up rods on the beach and hope for whiting, pompano, or bluefish. Or go up to the Flagler Beach pier. There is a boat launch on the Intracoastal Waterway.

It is just a short drive to the Bulow Plantation Ruins State Historic Site. Besides touring the ruins you can take the four-mile Bulow Woods Hiking Trail. It leads into a shady hammock among live oak trees and along Bulow Creek, passing near a marsh, then loops back to the parking area. Bulow Creek is a state-designated canoe trail. There is a landing at the state historic site and canoes are available at a modest rental. You can paddle upstream for three miles or head down six miles to the Intracoastal Waterway. The tidal marsh and surrounding lush woods make for a memorable paddle.

What's Nearby

Bulow Creek State Park is a must for Gamble Rogers visitors. I never pass up a chance for a visit. It is a forest enclave along the west shore of Bulow Creek. Here grows the Fairchild Oak, an example of an ideally shaped old growth live oak that has not fallen prey to development or fire over the years. A three-mile hiking trail connects the Fairchild Oak to the Bulow Woods Hiking Trail, making a six-mile one-way hike between the Fairchild Oak and the Bulow Plantation Ruins State Historic Site. I recommend that you make this hike during the cooler and drier winter months.

Information

Gamble Rogers Memorial State Recreation Area
3100 South US A1A
Flagler Beach, FL 32136
(386) 517-2086, www.floridastateparks.org; reservations (800) 326-3521, www.reserveamerica.com
Open: Year-round
Sites: 34
Amenities: Picnic table, fire ring, water, electricity
Registration: By phone or at park entrance booth
Facilities: Hot showers, flush toilets, pay phone
Fees: $23 per night
Directions: Gamble Rogers is on US A1A just south of the pier in the town of Flagler Beach.

Tomoka State Park

Ormond Beach, Florida

Tomoka has the good fortune of possessing one of the state's most attractive campgrounds and being located minutes away from the world-famous Daytona Beach. Tucked away on the north tip of the peninsula between the Halifax and Tomoka rivers, Tomoka State Park has a remote aura, yet it is within the boundaries of the city of Ormond Beach. The actual beaches at Ormond Beach and Daytona Beach are a ten-minute drive from your favorite campsite at Tomoka.

You'll have a difficult time picking out your favorite campsite. Mother Nature mixed a little north Florida with a little south Florida and placed the combination near the ocean to make a jungle-like forest that belies the true location of this suburban getaway. The Timucuan Indians thought highly of Tomoka Point as well. The village of Nocoroco stood here in pre-Columbian days. The natives lived off the rich estuarine waters of the surrounding lagoon. An onsite museum explains the history of the Timucuans, so you can enjoy a day at the beach and learn a little history too.

The Beach/Coast

Tomoka is surrounded on three sides by water. The Tomoka River flows from the west into Tomoka Basin, where it meets the Halifax River, which is

Figure 25. A lone kayaker in the Tomoka River at Tomoka State Park.

the body of water between the mainland and the barrier island at Ormond Beach. The peninsula where the state park lies has small barrier islands and inlets surrounding it, so most of your views are of nature, not condos. Off in the distance are grassy salt marshes and cedar- and palm-lined coast leading directly to the estuary, leaving just a short stretch of beach on the northwest end of the peninsula.

However, a short drive away on Granada Avenue is genuine Atlantic Ocean beach. Here you pass an access booth and turn right onto the beach. The light tan sands rise moderately from the ocean and then steepen into a bluff. Numerous houses, condos, and hotels are atop the bluff.

This Ormond Beach access is the first of several access points maintained by Volusia County. Farther south lies Daytona, arguably the world's most famous beach. Its reputation means it attracts beach lovers of all types, making Daytona a great beach to see humanity at play.

The Campground

Tomoka has a most attractive campground. Of course this is a matter of opinion, but if you like to camp where the natural world gets the emphasis and where campground amenities are unobtrusively integrated into a wooded setting, you'll agree with my opinion.

The backbone of the forest here is the live oak, with resurrection ferns and Spanish moss thriving on these host trees. Oak limbs stretch over the balance of the forest. RVers need to be apprised that these beautiful oaks restrict RV size to 34 feet in length and 11 feet in height. Palm trees mixed with the oaks add to the tropical jungle feel of Tomoka. Smaller scrub oaks fill in the woods, along with pine trees. The heavy understory allows campers ample privacy.

With the thickness of the vegetation, you can only see a few if any of your fellow campers, making the campground seem small. And after a sun-splashed day at the beach, I appreciate a shady campsite. Three bathhouses keep the walk from your tent or RV to the shower minimal. All campsites have water and electricity.

Tomoka is fairly quiet during January, with some snowbirds setting up camp. But in February, watch out. "Speed Week" during the Daytona 500 fills the campground. So does "Bike Week," when motorcycle enthusiasts fill the streets of nearby Daytona. Then the spring breakers come, though they usually won't fill the campground completely. Campsites are generally available during summer, barring major holidays. After September, business slows again until the cold weather infiltrates the northland. Any time of year is a good time to visit Tomoka.

Human and Natural History

The Timucuan Indians were among the first peoples to enter Florida over 14,000 years ago. A particular band of Timucuans settled on the western end of the peninsula that is Tomoka State Park today. Their village was known as Nocoroco. Here the Timucuans could harvest the rich waters of Tomoka Basin and be protected from hurricanes by the barrier island where Ormond Beach is today.

Oyster shell mounds and burial mounds at the park are important archaeological sites, some harboring a record dating back 7,000 years. Timucuan communities were often located within wooden walls not unlike those of a fort. Within the refuge was a central community house where the chief lived, with smaller huts of individual citizens nearby.

The sea was not their only food source. The Timucuans were skilled hunters with bow and arrow as well as using traps. Deer and small game complemented their seafood diet. European colonization of the area all but wiped out the Timucuans.

What to Do

As noted, Tomoka is just a short drive from either Ormond or Daytona Beach. At Ormond Beach you have the option of going to an auto-accessible beach or a foot-traffic-only beach. Either way, the Atlantic Ocean is beautiful and powerful, ebbing and flowing day and night, waiting patiently for your arrival. At Daytona Beach a wider variety of concessionaires rents out the equipment to ride personal watercraft, sail, surf, or whatever floats your body. The city of Daytona Beach also has all manner of tourist fun.

The wooded environment of Tomoka is extra-inviting after a day at the beach. Park rangers told me that relaxing at the campground is a time-honored pastime here. But keep in mind that Tomoka has a little waterfront of its own. Boating and paddling are popular in the Tomoka and Halifax rivers; there is a boat launch at the park. Sea trout, flounder, and snook inhabit these brackish depths.

However, swimming is not allowed at the park. What you can do is take a walk on the nature trail beginning near the park museum. The park museum interprets the rich human history that has played out on Tomoka Point. It also houses art works of Fred Dana Marsh, the sculptor of the "Legend of Tomokie" at the park. Marsh was a multitalented artist who settled in Ormond Beach in the 1920s. The sculpture was his last project.

What's Nearby

Since Tomoka is a suburban park, city life is close at hand. Any type of store or restaurant can be found nearby. In the search for seafood, follow this general rule: get as close to fishing villages or fishing boats as possible; if there are no fishing boats or villages nearby, then get as close to the ocean as possible. This axiom is not infallible, but it will help more than it hurts.

State holdings nearby include the ancient, near perfect live oak specimen called the Fairchild Oak, and the Bulow Plantation Ruins, site of a plantation and old sugar mill and worth the drive. Canoers can paddle three canoe trails: at Bulow Creek, Spruce Creek, or the upper reaches of the Tomoka River. The sights of Cape Canaveral Space Center and Cape Canaveral National Seashore are a reasonable drive to the south.

Information

Tomoka State Park
2099 North Beach Street
Ormond Beach, FL 32174
(904) 676-4050, www.floridastateparks.org; reservations (800) 326-3521, www.reserveamerica.com
Open: Year-round
Sites: 100
Amenities: Water, electricity, picnic table, fire ring
Registration: By Internet, phone, or at park entrance booth
Facilities: Hot showers, flush toilets, pay phone
Fees: $20 per night
Directions: From FL 40 in Ormond Beach turn north on Beach Street. Follow it for three miles to Tomoka State Park.

Anastasia State Recreation Area

St. Augustine, Florida

This state recreation area has three positive elements going for it: a very attractive campground set in a maritime hammock forest, miles of wide Atlantic beach, and proximity to the historic heart of America's oldest city, St. Augustine. Situated on Anastasia Island, across the Bridge of Lions from downtown St. Augustine, Anastasia lets you mix nature, a little watery recreation, and a trip through history without spending much time in your vehicle.

Set up camp beneath live oaks and magnolias in large campsites. Then walk to the beach, spread out your gear, and watch the waves roll in. After a day in the sun, head into St. Augustine for an evening walking tour and a nice dinner. Or just enjoy the evening at the campground, take a moonlit stroll on the beach, and see the historic sights of St. Augustine the next day.

The Beach/Coast

Four and a half miles of beach stretch along the northeastern tip of Anastasia Island. The most northerly point of the island overlooks the main entrance to St. Augustine Harbor. A jetty extends into the harbor pass and is popular with fishermen. Beyond the jetty is an inlet known as Salt Run, which has a small beach of its own.

Figure 26. Windswept oaks at Anastasia State Recreation Area.

Visitors get to the shoreline from the beach parking area at the southern end of the recreation area. All beach access at the park is by foot. No cars are allowed here, though cars are allowed on St. Augustine Beach to the south of the park. To the north begins the wide, gently sloping beach bordering the Atlantic Ocean, with the waves rolling in. Behind the beach are low dunes covered with sea oats. The first mile of beach is designated for swimmers only. The second mile of wide beach is the designated surfing area. The third and fourth miles of beach, where the dunes flatten out, are designated for fishermen and personal watercraft. This setup allows like-minded beach enthusiasts to be grouped together and minimizes conflicts.

In addition to this beach, there 42 miles more of beaches in St. Johns County. Nearby to the north are Vilano Beach; to the south are St. Augustine Beach, Butler Beach, Crescent Beach, and Guana River State Park. Guana River has both beach and bayfront water access. A spectacular wild beach is open to the public at Fort Matanzas about 10 miles south of Anastasia.

The Campground

The large Anastasia campground is spread out in a beautiful maritime hammock forest. Thousands of years ago, when the ocean was higher than it is today, the site of the campground was covered in sand dunes and sea oats. But the ocean retreated and the rolling dunes became wooded. Now the dominant tree, live oak, spreads its arms over southern magnolias, smaller oaks, cedar, palm, and a bushy, thick understory of yaupon, red bay, and young trees. Overhead the tree canopy is sculpted by the constant action of wind coming off the Atlantic, which is a few hundred yards distant, separated from the campground by Salt Run. Being spread over old dunes lends the campground a rolling nature.

Seven ovals filled with campsites run beneath the lush woods. The first loop, Coquina, is located away from the rest of the campground and has 33 campsites. The sites are large and attract primarily RV campers. All sites at Anastasia have water and electricity.

The other six loops are sand roads through attractive woods along the main campground road. Lush forest shades the sites, and bathhouses are easily accessible. These loops spread the campground over a wide area. The thick woods overhead and the understory between sites makes for a pleasant camping experience that is enhanced by the campground's cleanliness. All these factors make this an increasingly popular place to park your rig or pitch your tent. The off season is from October through February, but even then weekend nights can fill. Spring and summer are popular; Anastasia can be full every night during summer. Reservations are always recommended.

Human and Natural History

Established where Timucuan Indians were already living, St. Augustine has been under numerous flags during its long history. Don Pedro Menendez de Aviles of Spain founded St. Augustine in the year 1565. The English attacked it no less than four times. Their attacks prompted the erection of St. Augustine's famous Castillo de San Marcos, a fort twenty-three years in the making. In the 1702 attack the fort was the only thing that didn't fall to the British, who burned the rest of the city. In 1763 British efforts finally paid off when they got Florida from the Spaniards in exchange for Cuba.

The English ruled St. Augustine for only twenty years before it was returned to the Spaniards, and the United States got the Florida territory from the Spaniards in 1821. During the Civil War, Confederate and then Union forces occupied the fort and town.

After the war, oilman and Florida developer Henry Flagler came to St. Augustine, building grand hotels and churches, visualizing the town as a major winter resort. His architecture enhanced the old city before he moved farther south. In 1924 Castillo de San Marcos was designated a national monument, recognizing the historic value of the continent's oldest continuously occupied European settlement.

What to Do

The beach is the primary attraction at Anastasia. The sandy shoreline is wide and flat, allowing room for sunbathers aplenty beside the rolling Atlantic with its big waves. During the warmer months a concessionaire rents all sorts of equipment, such as volleyballs, sailboards, and paddleboats.

The Atlantic waves attract surfers to Anastasia. Personal watercraft are also enjoyed offshore. Fishermen can surf cast on the beach for bluefish or pompano or fish the quieter waters of Salt Run for flounder or redfish. Canoers, kayakers, and sailboarders likewise enjoy Salt Run.

Before walking around St. Augustine, walk the Ancient Sand Dunes Nature Trail and see what the area was like before the Spaniards arrived. When you get to St. Augustine, park near the visitor center and strike out from there. Cross the street and check out Castillo de San Marcos, the old Spanish fort. Then take one of the sightseeing trains for an overview of this old town.

Attractions are numerous and varied. See the oldest wooden schoolhouse, the Ripley's Believe It or Not Museum, or see the St. Augustine Alligator Farm, which has been there for more than a hundred years. Climb the St. Augustine Lighthouse for a panoramic view of the surrounding environs. Shoppers need to be restrained in St. Augustine. Shops and small galleries offer everything from crafts by skilled artisans to the cheapest plastic souvenirs.

What's Nearby

Beach lovers will want to explore the vast array of sandy shorelines extending both north and south. I highly recommend a trip south to Fort Matanzas National Monument. Not only does it have a pristine beach with dunes and sea oats; it also has a Spanish fort from the 1740s located out in the mouth of the Matanzas River, which was the back way into St. Augustine. A free national park ferryboat takes you out to the fort itself. Just south of Fort Matanzas lie the Washington Oaks State Gardens, nearly 400 acres of scenic rock-strewn beach and ornamental gardens.

Since Anastasia is so close to the town of St. Augustine, food, supplies, and entertainment venues are readily available no matter which way you turn. You'll probably end up doing a combination of sightseeing, shopping, and eating out in the true tourist style.

Information

Anastasia State Recreation Area
1340 A. US A1A South
St. Augustine, FL 32084
(904) 461-2033, www.floridastateparks.org; reservations (800) 326-3521, www.reserveamerica.com
Open: Year-round
Sites: 139
Amenities: Picnic table, fire ring, water, electricity
Registration: By phone, internet, or at park entrance booth
Facilities: Hot showers, flush toilets, pay phone, laundry
Fees: $23 per night
Directions: From St. Augustine, drive south on US A1A over the Bridge of Lions and go 4 miles. Anastasia State Recreation Area is on your left.

Little Talbot Island State Park
Fort George, Florida

Little Talbot Island is one of the largest undeveloped barrier islands in Florida. Located on the northeastern coast near Jacksonville, Little Talbot is one of the "Sea Islands of the South," which stretch northward up the coast into Georgia and South Carolina. These islands are characterized by wide sandy beaches along the Atlantic, thick maritime live oak hammocks on ancient dunes in the center, and grassy salt marshes cut by tidal streams dividing the islands from the mainland.

True to form, Little Talbot, part of the Talbot Islands State Park, is a gem. The beach is one of the most pristine in the South. The island's wooded center is jungle-like in its lushness. The grassy salt marsh is a scenic estuary where much of ocean life around here begins. Nearby, other islands such as Fort George and Big Talbot emphasize the historic importance and natural attractions of these Sea Islands. On Fort George, the remains of a cotton plantation and a missing military fort show the uses of barrier islands in the past. The incredible beauty of The Bluffs on Big Talbot Island completes the picture.

The Beach/Coast

Fort George River separates Little Talbot Island from Fort George Island to the south. The pass between these two islands is a widely fluctuating tidal

Figure 27. Driftwood at Little Talbot Island State Park. Photo by Doug Alderson.

flow that covers and exposes sand bars. Along the Atlantic side of Little Talbot are five miles of wide beach gently sloping up from the ocean. Due to the strong tides near the Fort George Inlet, swimming is wisely not allowed here. The beach area begins farther north. Two major parking and pavilion areas are connected to the beach by boardwalks. This strand is backed by sea oats–covered sand dunes that extend all the way to the north point of the island, which reaches Nassau Sound. Surfers favor the big waves near the point.

As you make your way back south around the island a grassy salt marsh begins. Simpson Creek is the main watercourse flowing among the grass. A boat launch and small sandy area are located near the park campground, then the marsh continues south to meet the Fort George River.

Just north of Little Talbot is Big Talbot Island. A stretch of the island fronts Nassau Sound. Here, tall bluffs drop straight off to a small beach littered with skeletons of live oaks that have fallen into the sea. Rock formations break out of the sand in places. You can look toward the salt marsh, or over at Little Talbot Island or beyond the shifting sand bars of the sound into the Atlantic. Bring your camera to this beautiful and different beach.

The Campground

This campground is attractive, and I get a feeling of everyone being in on the secret of having found this great place. Pass the locked gate from US A1A and enter the campground via a sandy road that winds behind some ancient sand dunes. These large dunes block much of the wind. The 40-site campground has two fully equipped bathhouses located between the three loops. Campsites vary in size; the park places visitors according to size of outfit. All the campsites have water and electricity. Shade is generally the rule, though there are some fairly sunny creekside campsites. Many campsites are beneath live oaks covered in ferns; others overlook the salt marsh. Come March, Little Talbot Island grows busy. You can count on it being filled nearly every weekend. During the week there are usually a few open spots. It's the same way through the summer, but don't be surprised if the campground fills on a weekday. The place clears in September, even though fall is a great time to visit. In the winter, Little Talbot really slows down. But on the first pretty weekend after a prolonged spell of bad weather, locals flood the campground. Campers consist of about half RVs and half tent campers throughout the year.

Human and Natural History

The restored Kingsley Plantation is on nearby Fort George Island. The famous Sea Island cotton was grown here. The cotton was especially high quality, and the flat seeds were more easily separated from the fiber in the days before the cotton gin. These two factors made Sea Island cotton the most profitable of all cottons to grow. However, cultivating the fiber was labor intensive. This was where slave labor was highly valued.

On the Kingsley Plantation are the remains of twenty-three of the original thirty-two slave cabins. Today you can see the cabins where these slaves lived. In the main house is a visitor center where artifacts found on the site are on display. The house offers a glimpse into the life of the plantation owner, Zephaniah Kingsley, who operated the plantation from 1813 to 1839. A man named McQueen first established the plantation in 1791.

In addition to Kingsley's home there is a restored barn on the site. As you drive away, imagine the sandy road as it was, an avenue with mature palm trees lining the road that ran through cleared fields growing Sea Island cotton.

What to Do

The Talbot Islands are oriented toward nature lovers. The sandy oceanside is a fine place to go beachcombing. The gradual changes of depth along the oceanfront make for good swimming opportunities. The farther north you head, the more isolated the beach becomes. Combine the beach with the woods by taking the Little Talbot Island Hiking Trail through a lush maritime forest for 2.5 miles, passing some big dunes just before reaching the beach. The Campground Nature Trail, which runs along an inlet of the Fort George River, makes for a good warmup walk.

Paddling is popular on the landward side of the island. Myrtle and Simpson creeks are paddling wildlife observation venues in this grassy estuary. Long Island Outfitters offers canoes and kayaks for rent to explore the salt marsh creeks. You can also bring your rod and fish for sea trout, redfish, and flounder. Surf fishermen cast in the Atlantic for bigger species.

Birdwatchers scan for the 194 species of birds known to inhabit the beaches, dunes, and estuaries of the park. Armadillos, raccoons, deer, rabbits, and bobcats call this place home. Another must visit for nature lovers is the Black Rock Trail on Big Talbot Island. Walk through a level forest of live oak to

The Bluffs. Descend onto the beach and explore the environs around Nassau Island. This is a great place to watch the sun rise or set.

What's Nearby

More area state parks and with Timucuan Ecological and Historic Preserve offer multiple excursion opportunities. Fort George Island is four miles south of Little Talbot on US A1A. There you can walk, drive, or bike the 4.4-mile Saturiwa Trail. An old sandy road that makes a loop, this trail explores the human and natural history of the island. Twenty-eight marked sites explain the periods of occupation from the time of the Saturiwa Indians to the plantation era to modern times. The highlight of the loop is the Kingsley Plantation. Anglers can enjoy the George Grady Bridge fishing pier between Amelia Island and Big Talbot Island. Nearby on the mainland, Pumpkin Hill Creek Preserve State Park offers multiple-use trails within its 4,000 acres. Amelia Island State Park, with horse rentals, offers a chance to ride horses on the beach.

Information

Little Talbot Island State Park
12157 Heckshear Drive
Fort George, FL 32226
(904) 251-2320, www.floridastateparks.org; reservations (800) 326-3521, www.reserveamerica.com
Open: Year-round
Sites: 40
Amenities: Picnic table, fire ring, water, electricity
Registration: By phone or at park entrance booth
Facilities: Hot showers, flush toilets, pay phone
Fees: $19 per night
Directions: From exit 358 on I-95 in Jacksonville, take FL 105 north (Heckshear Drive) for 22 miles to Little Talbot Island State Park, which will be on your right. FL 105 turns into US A1A after passing the ferry to Mayport a few miles before Little Talbot Island.

Fort Clinch State Park

Fernandina Beach, Florida

Why should a beach camper come to Fort Clinch State Park? To see a restored brick fort, camp in either of two appealing yet diverse campgrounds, and enjoy three types of marine environments: the Atlantic Ocean, Cumberland Sound, and the Amelia River. Fort Clinch is located on the northern tip of Amelia Island, which happens to be the most northeasterly spot in Florida. Here the Atlantic Ocean gives way to Cumberland Sound and the Amelia River.

History buffs, fishermen, hikers, mountain bikers, and beachgoers all enjoy this park. Reenactments and candlelight tours are held at the fort, which is open daily for exploration. There are several different ways to fish here. The ultralong park pier is just one way to pursue big fish. Hikers and bikers can enjoy a newly constructed path that winds among old forested sand dunes. And the beach can be just as relaxing as either of the two campgrounds.

The Beach/Coast

Nearly a mile of beachfront looks out over the Atlantic Ocean. The sand is tan and gently sloping. Sunbathers bask and swimmers cool off in the waves.

Figure 28. Fort Clinch was strategically positioned for defensive purposes but is now scenically located on the edge of Cumberland Sound.

A jetty first built during the Spanish American War in 1898, and rebuilt since then, extends over a mile into the Atlantic. This makes the sand extend out into a point before turning beyond the jetty. Ocean lovers and anglers enjoy a 2,000-foot pier along the jetty.

As the shore turns west into Cumberland Sound dangerous currents mean swimming is prohibited, but beachcombing is welcomed along the 1.5 miles of beach that abut the sound. The beach is not as wide here as on the Atlantic shore. Erosion-inhibiting rocks indicate the beginning of Fort Clinch. Cumberland Island and Georgia are across the sound.

The coast turns back south as you pass a small fishing deck and boat ramp. Here the Amelia River is wider than the sound was. However, the beach has narrowed and the shoreline slopes sharply. Red cedars and live oaks grow close to the water. The Amelia River narrows, then gives way to Egans Creek, which is a classic Sea Islands tidal creek flowing amid grassy marsh.

Other nearby beaches on Amelia Island are Fernandina Beach, run by the city of Fernandina Beach; American Beach with its big dunes; and Amelia Island State Recreation Area, where you can rent horses and ride them on the beach.

The Campground

There are two distinctly different campgrounds at Fort Clinch. Atlantic Beach Campground is the domain of the RVs. It is located behind a series of oceanside dunes. The simple oval design features all 21 campsites on the outside of the oval. A brick bathhouse centers the oval and a boardwalk leads to the beach. A few palm trees provide the only shade. The minimal vegetation has its advantages, among them an ocean breeze that reduces insects. The view of the surrounding sand dunes is nice, too. But that ocean breeze in winter will also keep you in your RV.

Amelia River Campground, bordering a coastal marsh, offers a different atmosphere. The 41 mostly large campsites are set in a lush shady coastal hammock forest of live oak draped in Spanish moss, an occasional magnolia, and some of many large mature red cedar trees. The understory is primarily yaupon, red bay, and palmetto. Two brick comfort stations serve the campground. This campground is cooler in the summer but a few extra bugs are the price you pay.

Fort Clinch has been growing in popularity; there used to be a distinct off season in the coolest months. Don't be misled—now the campground fills on winter weekends. After March it can be full any day of the week, and on summer weekends it will be full. Business slows somewhat after Labor Day and campsites can be had any day except for nice Saturdays.

Human and Natural History

Fort Clinch began to take shape in 1842 when the United States government purchased the north end of Amelia Island for a military installation as part of a program to protect our country's seaports. Fort Clinch was only partially completed by the Civil War. That is why different colored bricks are in the fort. The first bricks came from Georgia, but after the conflict began, shipments stopped. The top bricks were shipped from New York. The Confederates were first in possession of the fort during wartime. But the Union captured several forts up the coast, leaving Fort Clinch isolated, so the Confederates abandoned it.

Construction was renewed after the Yankees took over but was not completed even after war's end. The fort was then deactivated until the Spanish American War in 1898. The bastion soon resumed its slow deterioration. The fort was used once more during World War II as a Coast Guard surveillance post. By this time it had passed from the federal government to private hands and then to the state of Florida. In the state's hands Fort Clinch became one of Florida's first state parks. The Civilian Conservation Corps developed much of the park during the Great Depression. It has been well taken care of ever since.

What to Do

A tour of the fort is mandatory. See the cannons, the jail, the officers' quarters, and the courtyard. You may be one of the lucky ones who sees the fort come alive during a reenactment. These take place during the first weekend of every month and on special occasions. Rangers and volunteers dress in costume from the 1860s and live life as it was during that time, going about their chores. They answer your questions about what they are up to, but they know nothing of life after the 1860s. Special candlelight tours are held during summer. If you miss one of these events, tour the fort anyway; the views from the top are spectacular.

The beach is a year-round attraction, even if sunbathing and swimming are a warmer-month proposition. Ecotourists go shelling and birdwatching. One can walk the beach along the sound and along Amelia River. Fishing can be done in the surf, from the pier, or from a boat put out from the boat launch; sheepshead and whiting are likely pier catches, while redfish and sea trout are caught in the Amelia River.

Bicyclists can tool the main park roads, and mountain bikers have an additional treat in store for them—a six-mile trail that winds among the ancient sand dunes of the island interior. Hikers can also enjoy this trail and the foot-only Willow Pond Nature Trail.

What's Nearby

On the south end of Amelia Island is Amelia Island State Recreation Area. This is one of the few places left on the East Coast where you can ride horses on the beach. Rides are made by reservation. Call (904) 491-5166 for reservations.

The town of Fernandina Beach has a restored historic district. There are coffee shops, antique stores, and homes that hark back to another time. You have to drive through town to get to Fort Clinch, so you can weigh your options during the drive.

Information

Fort Clinch State Park
2601 Atlantic Avenue
Fernandina Beach, FL 32034
(904) 277-7274, www.floridastateparks.org; reservations (800) 326-3521, www.reserveamerica.com
Open: Year-round
Sites: 62
Amenities: Picnic table, fire ring, water, electricity
Registration: By phone or at park entrance booth
Facilities: Hot showers, flush toilets, laundry, pay phone
Fees: $23
Directions: From the town of Fernandina Beach, drive east on US A1A for one mile. Fort Clinch State Park is on your left.

Georgia

Cumberland Island National Seashore
St. Marys, Georgia

The only way to get to Cumberland Island is by boat. But don't let this little impediment stop you. A ferry offers regular service from the nearby coastal town of St. Marys. Once you arrange your boat ride and debark on this tranquil barrier island, the southernmost in the Peach State, you will appreciate the slow pace, auto-free setting, and some of the best scenery in the Southeast. Windswept beaches lead up to wooded dunes, behind which massive live oaks shade palmetto thickets. It's a place where wild horses roam the woods and sands, where historic mansions and ruins of mansions add human history to the natural beauty. It's a place where the four seasons offer distinctive experiences that will make you want to return time and again.

Figure 29. A campsite beneath the live oaks on Cumberland Island.

From your overnighting base, known as Sea Camp, you can explore this federally designated national seashore on foot, just relax on the beach, or attend National Park Service interpretive programs delving into the story of Cumberland Island.

The Beach/Coast

Cumberland Island is a north-south-oriented barrier island facing the Atlantic Ocean. The Atlantic side of the island is primarily beach all the way from the Florida border, just across the mouth of the St. Marys River, north to Sea Camp Beach, accessible from the campground. Continuing north, you pass Little Greyfield Beach and Stratford Beach, which is near a backcountry camping site. Farther north, you reach the wilderness area of the island. The northernmost spot on its Atlantic shore is known as Long Point. The Atlantic side features nearly 15 miles of beachfront.

The landward side of the island is more estuarine in character. Salt marsh is cut by tidal channels. The Cumberland River is the primary waterway between the mainland and Cumberland Island. The national seashore visitor access area is on the south end of the island. This is where the ferry lands and unloads visitors, and where campers muster their gear for transport to the Atlantic side of Cumberland Island. There is also dock space for private boats. The park ranger station, a museum, and the ruins of the mansion Dungeness are located here.

The Campground

Before you can set out for the Sea Camp campground, you attend a short ranger orientation. Then you can get a campsite and load your equipment onto carts provided by the park service for hauling gear the few hundred yard from the dock to the camp.

Sea Camp lies in a live oak forest beside dunes leading to the Atlantic. Massive tree trunks branch and reach outward, their long limbs dripping with Spanish moss. Palmetto and wax myrtle bushes grow under the oaks. The campsites are literally cut out from the brush. Each campsite has elevated food storage boxes. The raccoons here are particularly adept at getting human food, so the park service installed these boxes for every camper's use. Most sites are heavily shaded and large enough to accommodate whatever supplies you can bring on the ferry. Be prepared before arriving, as there are no stores on the island and you must bring all the supplies you need. You must also pack out all your trash. The campground does provide water. A bathhouse near the center has cold indoor showers and flush toilets. Outdoor showers are available near the boardwalk to the beach.

This campground is popular. Business is steady year-round despite the heat and bugs of summer and sporadic cold snaps of winter. With its limited number of sites, this campground is likely to fill almost every weekend of the year except in bad weather. Reservations can be made six months in advance and are highly recommended. In summer, the stays are generally shorter than the seven-day limit. In winter the ferry doesn't run on Monday or Tuesday, altering visitation patterns a little.

Human and Natural History

Cumberland Island was named for the Duke of Cumberland during the 1700s after the Spanish abandoned the island. They had established Fort San Pedro to counter the French, who had already dispatched the Indians. Georgia's founder, James Oglethorpe, established better forts on the island, but none of the defenses saw action. In the early 1800s Nathaneal Greene started a summer home called Dungeness; he soon died and the home was finished by his wife but later burned. Magnate Andrew Carnegie built a lavish home upon the ruins in the late 1800s. At one time Carnegie owned nearly the entire island and had a staff of three hundred just to maintain his place! You can still see what is left of Dungeness, but you will have to visit Cumberland Island to learn what happened to Carnegie's estate.

What to Do

Nearly every barrier island in Georgia has been or is being developed, so the natural beach is a big draw. Cumberland Island does have some private inholdings, but most of it is in nature's hands. The beach compares favorably to any other on the East Coast. The interior of the island is beautiful as well. Live oaks and pine woods are divided by wetlands and inland ponds. Miles and miles of trails traverse the island from one end to the other. Wild horses roam Cumberland Island, and visitors always want to see them.

Close to Sea Camp the River Trail leads south from the park office to the Dungeness Dock and the Dungeness Historic District. This historic area is the site of two former mansions, both with this mysterious name. There are more than ruins here, but you will have to explore for yourself and learn of a way of life gone by. Better yet, join a ranger for one of the twice-daily interpretive walks. The upper end of the island has Plum Orchard, an intact mansion, and The Settlement. Park tours of Plum Orchard and The Settlement are held monthly.

What's Nearby

Since Cumberland Island is a barrier island, it is an all-inclusive experience. Another outdoor venue nearby is the St. Marys River, excellent for canoeing. You can start at its outflow from the Okefenokee Swamp and paddle for more than 50 miles to Folkston, Georgia. This beautiful blackwater stream is bordered by blinding white sandbars and stately cypress trees. Intrepid paddlers continue downstream to the town of St. Marys, in the tidal portion of the river. The Okefenokee Swamp is a destination in itself. Take a guided boat tour of the Okefenokee National Wildlife Refuge or rent a boat of your own. Hiking trails and a wildlife observation drive round out what the Okefenokee offers.

Information

Cumberland Island National Seashore
P.O. Box 806
St. Marys, GA 31558
(912) 882-4336, www.nps.gov/cuis, camping reservations (912) 882-4335; ferry reservations (888) 817-3421, call M–F, 10 a.m.–4 p.m.
Open: Year-round
Sites: 16
Amenities: Picnic table, fire ring, raccoon-proof food storage box, trash storage pole
Registration: At camper check-in station on Cumberland Island
Facilities: Cold indoor and outdoor showers, flush toilets, water spigots
Fees: $4 per person per night
Directions: From exit 3 on I-95, take GA 40 east for 10 miles to dead end in St. Marys near the park visitor center and private ferry. You then take the ferry to Cumberland Island.

Fort McAllister State Park

Richmond Hill, Georgia

The camping area at Fort McAllister is on Savage Island, one of the Sea Islands sprinkled along the coast of Georgia. Here the Ogeechee River nears the ocean, and during the Civil War its bluffs became a place of importance for the Confederacy to defend nearby Savannah from attack by the Union. Times were mostly quiet on the banks of the Ogeechee. However, Fort McAllister was the last stop during Sherman's March to the Sea, which essentially ended the Civil War. Later Henry Ford bought the land and preserved the fort's earthworks, which eventually led to its designation as a historical site and its becoming part of the Georgia state park system. Today you can tour the fort, explore the waterways of the Ogeechee River and the history of the greater Savannah area, then return to your camp on Savage Island at the end of the road, a quiet haven for RVs and tent campers alike.

The Beach/Coast

The shoreline here is dominated by the Ogeechee River, making its final bends before opening into Ossabow Sound and the Atlantic Ocean. Much

Figure 30. Fort McAllister State Park has a rich history, depicted at its museum.

of the park and the actual Fort McAllister are set on the south bank of the Ogeechee, which runs wide here and is heavily influenced by the tides. A sweep of low-lying cordgrass extends beyond the north bank of the river, allowing vistas that extend far into the distance. The fort itself is at a place known as Genesis Point. This bluff allows long views up and down the river, which made it a great place for a defensive garrison. A fine-looking picnic area shaded by pines and live oaks lies upstream of the fort, overlooking the Ogeechee. A fishing pier also reaches into the water here. A bridge leads one mile from the fort area to Savage Island, where campers can enjoy overnight stays in lush woodland encircled by salt marsh and bordered by Redbird Creek. Redbird Creek offers water access into the Ogeechee River and ultimately the Atlantic for those so inclined. Be apprised that there is no direct beach access from here; the nearest public beach access is at least an hour's drive away, on Tybee Island.

The Campground

Savage Island, where the Fort McAllister camping area lies, is attached to the mainland by a causeway traversing the salt marsh and creeks that encircle the island. The dead-end causeway cuts down on traffic, making for a peaceful and serene camping experience at this island getaway. Overhead are wide-reaching live oaks, sweet magnolias, sturdy laurel oaks, pines, and palms. Spanish moss clings to the trees and sways in the summer breeze.

The campground is laid out in a grand loop cut by crossroads. The first camping area has sites #1–#18, plus the campground host. These shady pull-through sites are large but are not leveled, so a big RV rig will need leveling. The first crossroad, Raccoon Way, has sites #19–#38, also well shaded and catering to the big rigs. The sites are the smallest of the RV sites, however. The better crossroad is Armadillo Avenue, which houses the extremely large sites #44–#52; the biggest of RVs can light here, again under tall trees. The separate tent campers' area is at the farthest end of the island, on Deer Run. The sites become more heavily shaded as you proceed down Deer Run. All the sites are large here, too. Reservations are recommended on all holiday weekends from St. Patrick's Day through Thanksgiving. Campsites are generally available otherwise. The park also has one primitive campsite accessible by foot and one primitive campsite accessible by boat. A fire ring is the only amenity at these sites.

Human and Natural History

Fort McAllister was the most southerly of Savannah's defenses. At the outset of the Civil War Robert E. Lee, then in charge of the lower coast area, came to Fort McAllister and recommended improvements to the fort. His ideas proved helpful, as the fort was bombed by Union ironclad boats and other ships. Its sandy walls absorbed the impact of newer, heavy artillery shells and could be rebuilt overnight rather than crumbling under pressure, as the brick forts were doing. However, battles were few and far between—the men of the garrison mostly battled boredom. Officers kept strict discipline and kept the soldiers as busy as possible.

Fort McAllister dueled with the ironclad *Montauk* on several occasions, mostly to a draw. Finally Sherman decided to attack the fort by land, as it stood between him and the capture of Savannah. It wasn't long before the 230 Union men stormed the moat and earthworks of Fort McAllister and took over. The Rebels withdrew from Savannah, and Sherman had his prize.

What to Do

My first suggestion is to tour Fort McAllister and the adjacent museum. The views from the fort are inspiring and so is the setting, beneath the live oaks that grow on the earthworks. Times were different when soldiers manned the lonely outpost. Take note of how the soldiers used the material on hand for state-of-the-art sand fortifications. Check out the gun emplacements, massive earthworks, and underground quarters called "bombproofs."

After a historical tour, try the natural pursuits on beautiful Savage Island. The Magnolia Nature Trail starts near the end of the tent area and loops back to the campground. Paddlers can ply marsh-bordered Redbird Creek. The park rents out kayaks and canoes at reasonable rates; try to work routes to put the tides in your favor. The launch is open to bigger boats, too. If you want to pedal instead of paddle, rent a bike. The flat, quiet park roads are ideal for bicycling, especially on the causeway overlooking the expansive marshes. Bikers and hikers can also check out the Redbird Trail system back on the mainland. A series of interconnected loops traverses the rich forest and marshland protected by the park.

Fishing is always a possibility at Fort McAllister, as the soldiers also found. Try the dock and boat ramp near the campground or the 90-foot fishing pier on the Ogeechee River for whiting, sea trout, drum, and even sharks.

What's Nearby

Fort Pulaski National Monument, also a Civil War fort, is within striking distance. It is near Tybee Island, which as noted is also where the nearest beach to Fort McAllister is located. Fort Pulaski is run by the National Park Service. Here improved Union artillery rendered obsolete the long-held brick fortresses along the ocean. The Confederates quickly lost Fort Pulaski and the Union commander, David Hunter, took over the fort and freed slaves in the area. This fort is part of a 5,000-acre parcel preserving the beauty of the Sea Islands of Georgia. See the park staff at Fort McAllister for directions to Fort Pulaski National Monument. Historic Savannah can also be visited from Fort McAllister.

Information

Fort McAllister State Park
3894 Fort McAllister Road
Richmond Hill, GA 31324
(912) 727-2339, www.gastateparks.org; reservations (800) 864-7275 or www.gastateparks.org
Open: Year-round
Sites: 52 water and electric sites, 12 tent-only sites
Amenities: Picnic table, fire grate, water, electricity; tent sites also have tent pad
Registration: By phone, Internet, or at park entrance booth
Facilities: Hot showers, flush toilets, laundry, phone
Fees: RV or pop-up $20 per night, tent $18 per night
Directions: From exit 90 on I-95, take GA 144 east for 6.6 miles to GA 144 Spur. Turn left on GA 144 Spur and follow it 4 miles to the state park.

Skidaway Island State Park
Savannah, Georgia

If you want to combine camping out with exploring Savannah, consider staying at Skidaway Island State Park. It is located just south of the city on one of Georgia's barrier Sea Islands. The camping area is large and attractive and is a destination in its own right. The park itself is a compact 553 acres and is nearly surrounded by urban development, but if you are looking to mix civilization with a preserved parcel of what the Georgia coast was once like, then this is the place for you. It is an area where fresh water mixes with salt water, where low marshes border dense woodland. Campers who are history buffs like to visit Savannah, which has one of the largest historic preservation districts in the country. Colonial and Civil War history converge in this coastal town that played such a critical role in Georgia's past. The town is well aware of its history, and the Savannah River area is a treat to see.

The Beach/Coast

Skidaway Island is a barrier island that lies between Savannah and the Atlantic Ocean. Other barrier islands to the east are part of the Wassaw National Wildlife Refuge. The amount of shoreline in and around this park is its weak

Figure 31. RV camps in the pines on Skidaway Island.

link. There simply is not much of it. The park is small to begin with, and as indicated, beyond its borders the city has taken over much of the island. The west side of the park, however, is bordered by a stretch of the Skidaway River known as the Skidaway Narrows. The Intracoastal Waterway goes through here. Park trails travel to the Skidaway River and are the only way to get near it. Attractive coastal areas to visit outside the park are the downtown Savannah riverfront and Tybee Island, which has a beach in a region of limited beaches.

The Campground

This campground is a great spring and fall destination. It is set in a pretty forest of fern-covered live oaks, tall pines, and palms draped in Spanish moss. Yaupon, wax myrtle, and palmetto form brush borders between many campsites. The 88 sites are spread over such a wide area that you may get lost driving on the winding roads. Get a campground map when you arrive at the park entrance station.

All sites are pull-through, making life easy for RVers. The sites are mostly level, but parking pads are dirt or gravel. They are also widely separated, allowing for privacy and spaciousness. Three comfort stations are conveniently located in the campground. Sites #41–#65 are of special note, offering lush vegetation along a creek. They are also lower lying, but tent pads will keep you high and dry during the wettest times. Big rigs and tents scatter throughout the campground.

The campground fills on holiday weekends from St. Patrick's Day through Thanksgiving. Make reservations well in advance if you are coming then. Otherwise sites are generally available. Spring and fall are the busiest and best times to visit.

Human and Natural History

Have you ever seen a 20-foot-tall ground sloth? This was the tallest land mammal that ever lived. More than 10,000 years ago ground sloths fed on tree vegetation of the coastal plain of what became Georgia. In 1823 slaves of an area planter named Stark alerted him to some large and odd bones. Thanks to these bones Skidaway Island became known as the place of the giant sloth. Today at the interpretive center you can see a replica of this skeleton and learn about life in the day of the giant sloth, among other interesting things.

What to Do

The park does offer a swimming pool for those who want water to be part of their coastal camping experience. Other than the pool, which is open from Memorial Day through Labor Day, the rest of the park pursuits are nature oriented. Birding is popular here and the interpretive museum offers an introduction to birding. The painted bunting is an especially attractive bird that may be seen at Skidaway. A spotting scope is trained on a feeder just outside the museum. Binoculars, bird books, and taped bird songs help you get started. Then you can take off on the five miles of trails at the park and do a little birding on your own. The Sandpiper Trail travels through several ecosystems. Smaller birds may be out along Avian Way. Larger shorebirds may be out by the Skidaway Narrows. Along the trail are Confederate earthworks built to defend the waterway during the Civil War. (Short on defenses, the South may have used what were known as "Quaker cannons" to deter the Union: soldiers cut down palm trees and painted them to look like cannons, providing a mirage of increased defense.) An observation tower offers good views of the salt marsh.

The Big Ferry Interpretive Trail is longer and departs from near the campground. See more Confederate earthworks and the moonshine still from Prohibition days. Travel a boardwalk over a freshwater marsh and consider what life was like back when the Old Ferry Road led to a landing where locals would boat to Savannah to trade.

What's Nearby

The city of Savannah is just a short drive away. It is Georgia's first city and the former capital of one of our country's first thirteen states. History is everywhere you turn. See historic Civil War–era Fort Pulaski or Fort McAllister to the south, or visit the downtown riverfront with its restored old buildings. Certain sites are worth a tour, such as Wormsloe, the home of colonial settler Noble Jones. He arrived in 1733 to carve out a life on the Isle of Hope in what was then a howling wilderness. Consider visiting the King-Tisdell Cottage or other sites. Or board a boat and tour the area by water on the Savannah River.

Information

Skidaway Island State Park
52 Diamond Causeway
Savannah, GA 33043
(912) 598-2300, www.gastateparks.org; reservations (800) 864-7275, www.
gastateparks.org
Open: Year-round
Sites: 88
Amenities: Picnic table, fire grate, tent pad, water, electricity, cable hookup
Registration: By phone, Internet, or at park entrance booth
Facilities: Hot showers, flush toilets, laundry, pay phone
Fees: RV $24 per night, tent $22 per night
Directions: From exit 94 on I-95, take GA 204 east for 10.5 miles, then turn right on GA 204 Spur. Stay with GA 204 Spur for 7 miles and turn left onto the signed park road, soon to enter the park.

South Carolina

Hunting Island State Park
Beaufort, South Carolina

Hunting Island State Park has a beautiful landmark, the Hunting Island Lighthouse. This beacon stands tall on the park's four-mile stretch of preserved coastline fronting the Atlantic Ocean. Not only is the lighthouse pic-

Figure 32. Great views await from the top of Hunting Island Lighthouse.

turesque; the coastline is too. Live oaks, pines, and palms grow close to the shore. Skeletons of fallen trees meld into the sand. The Atlantic extends to the horizon. Assets besides the park's natural shoreline are the landscape of its lushly wooded interior and the marshes on its landward side. The campground here is large but is a good, shady destination for enjoying the offerings of this state park by the sea.

The Beach/Coast

Hunting Island forms the southernmost rampart fronting the Coosaw River as it flows into the Atlantic Ocean. The open water of St. Helena Sound lies to the north. To the east is the big Atlantic Ocean. The four miles of park beachfront reach from Hunting Island's northern tip south to Pritchard's Island, which also fronts the Atlantic. Hunting Island Beach runs along the Atlantic with enough sand to wear out the strongest pair of legs. The campground adjoins the beach on the most northerly part of Hunting Island. It is but a short walk from camp to the island's northernmost point. The Hunting Island Lighthouse is an easy walk south of the campground. It has appealing grounds and you can climb the lighthouse for a great view of your sandy empire. Moving south, several beach accesses lead from shady parking areas through the woods to the ocean. Farther south yet, privately owned cabins and park-owned cabins are near the ocean, but visitors can walk to the south tip of the island. The landward side of the island is marshy and includes the park's boat ramp, a boardwalk through the marsh, and a wildlife viewing area.

The Campground

The wooded setting of the spread-out campground is very pretty. Campers overnight beneath tall trees along the Atlantic shoreline. The first loop has campsites #1–#59. Live oaks, palms, and slash pines shade the oceanside sites. RVs primarily occupy this area. If you are going to camp here, go for sites #38–#55. They are within feet of the beach. The second beachfront loop has campsites #60–#86, also heavily shaded, with more pines than live oaks. Pine needles, oak leaves, and sand carpet the campsites.

In the rear camping area are campsites #89–#200 in a series of loops. If you value privacy, camp here. The woods are thicker, and ancient wooded dunes offer geographic relief in this section. Palmetto and brush add to the privacy.

This rear area also has the two walk-in tent camping areas, where solitude and quiet reign. The path to the first walk-in area, with sites T-1 through T-5, leaves the main campground near campsite #162. A sandy track leads to a heavily wooded rolling area, so hilly that tent sites are limited. Some sites have a fire grate in addition to a picnic table. The second walk-in tent camping area, near campsite #177, has sites T-6 through T-10. These are the best tent sites. They are more widespread, larger, and have more level ground among the trees.

Eight bathhouses are spread through the campground, and a camp store is located at the entrance. The campground fills every weekend during summer and occasionally during the week. Campsites #1–#40 are reservable; otherwise try to get here early on a Thursday to snag a site through the weekend. The walk-in sites fill on holiday weekends but are available on any weekday. Be prepared for mosquitoes after rainy periods.

Human and Natural History

The Hunting Island Lighthouse was built in 1873. It replaced one that was built in 1859 but dismantled by the Confederates to confound Union ships offshore as they plied the shoals that mark the halfway point between Savannah, Georgia, and Charleston, South Carolina. The light was moved to its present location in 1889, due to erosion, and was in use until 1933. The lives of the lighthouse keepers are detailed at the park. It was a lonely job with little contact between the folks who lived on this once remote barrier island and the rest of the world. Supply boats bringing the mail and the news highlight of the keeper's life.

What to Do

At 5,000 acres this state park is one of the largest in the South Carolina system. Its miles of beachfront attract many visitors to Hunting Island. Here you can while away the day at a setting free of the high-rises and commercialism of many other beach destinations. Most visitors walk south from the campground to see the Hunting Island Lighthouse, enjoy the view from the top of it, and learn about the history of the light and its keepers. Another way to enjoy the ocean is fishing. Surf fish on the beach or from the 1,120-foot pier extending into Fripp Island Inlet for whiting, speckled trout, drum, or flounder.

Eight miles of trails wind through the inland forest. In addition to the trail from the campground access road to the lighthouse area, another path makes a six-mile loop to the end of the island by the fishing pier and back. The mainland side of the park features a boardwalk through an estuarine marsh and has a wildlife viewing area. The park also offers a mountain bike trail.

What's Nearby

Its long beach makes Hunting Island a destination in itself. Of interest nearby is the small and historic town of Beaufort, founded well before the nation was founded. Take a buggy tour and see antebellum homes or learn about the Gullah culture of the Lowcountry, as the coastal area of South Carolina is known.

Visit the Beaufort Museum, or the Parris Island Museum, or the John Mark Verdier House. There are many other structures from the late 1700s and early 1800s to see while learning about the history of this coastal town.

Information

Hunting Island State Park
2555 Sea Island Parkway
Hunting Island, SC 29920
(843) 838-2011, www.southcarolinaparks.com; reservations (866) 345-PARK, www.southcarolinaparks.com
Open: Year-round
Sites: 173 water and electric, 10 walk-in tent campsites
Amenities: Water, electricity, picnic table, grill; walk-in tent sites have picnic table, grill, water spigot nearby
Registration: By phone, Internet, or at park entrance booth
Facilities: Hot showers, flush toilet, water spigots
Fees: Standard sites $23–25 per night, walk-in tent sites $17–19 March–November; rates are lower in the off season
Directions: From exit 33 on I-95, take US 21 south for 42 miles, through the town of Beaufort, and stay with US 21 to Hunting Island. Turn left on Campground Road to reach the campground.

Huntington Beach State Park

Murrells Inlet, South Carolina

Huntington Beach is a large oceanside park and camping area that is within striking distance of Myrtle Beach. This is not a remote park—far from it. However, Huntington Beach does offer a large campground, plenty of beachfront, and some history. In the park lies Atalaya, the winter home of the Huntington family, from whom the state acquired this property as well as Brookgreen Gardens on the mainland side of US 17. A look around will show you why the Huntingtons picked this part of South Carolina. Their home and your camping home are just inland from the pounding Atlantic Ocean, where the beach rises to dunes then dips back to a rich forest in places and attractive grounds in other places.

The Beach/Coast

This 2,500-acre park has three miles of ocean frontage. The Atlantic rolls into the sandy coastline, the beach rising to form sea oats–covered dunes. The

Figure 33. Atalaya is the preserved home at Huntington Beach State Park.

most northerly part of the park is marked by a jetty 1.2 miles beyond the most northerly beach access, a boardwalk leading from a picnic area with restrooms. Heading south from here, you are on North Beach. Next come two beach accesses that cut across the dunes and connect the campground to the ocean, making it easy for campers to reach the beach. There are two covered picnic shelters near these access points. The main day use area is a little farther south, and the primary office, store, and camper registration area is farthest back from the water. Beside the main parking area is a pleasant picnic spot with open tables and shady shelters. Cedars and palms grow on the grounds. A large elevated restroom and changing area are here, too. A wooden walkway leads over the dunes to the water.

The Huntington home Atalaya stands next to the day use area. The grounds and building are just back from the ocean, and the palm trees of the center court rise above the roof of the building. A line of trees stands between Atalaya and the ocean. Continuing south, the beach extends to the park boundary.

The Campground

The campground, a short walk from the beach, has two large loops with a separate walk-in tent camping area. The first loop, which has water, electricity, and sewer hookups, has the sites closest to the beach in a mix of sun and shade from planted cedars and live oaks. These first 40 sites are popular with RVers and are reservable. Make reservations for odd-numbered campsites #1–#31 in this loop. A recreation building is located near campsite #19 and is convenient for those inevitable summer thunderstorms. The first loop has two crossroads, too. Unless you have a hard-sided rig, avoid sites #74–#88 and #90–#102 on these crossroads: they are very open sites. Most sites on the remainder of the first loop have at least one shade tree. The second loop has sites farther from the ocean, most of them bordered with thick brush for campsite privacy.

Tent campers enjoy the walk-in tent sites. Leave the walk-in parking area and follow a sandy trail past a water spigot to the sites. They are shaded by live oaks and pines. Privacy is good back here, as brush thrives between the campsites.

This popular state park stays busy throughout the warmer part of the year. That means it fills at weekends from March to September and on many weekdays during the peak of summer. Campers crave the beachside sites, and exposure to an ocean breeze cuts down on insects when they are bothersome, usually following rainy periods.

Human and Natural History

Back in 1930 Archer and Anna Huntington were traveling the Intracoastal Waterway and came upon the property that is now the state park. The New Yorkers bought the 5,000 acres on the spot and began building a house as a wintering locale. They also wanted to preserve the area's natural attributes, from the open beach to the inland forests and the even larger area now called Brookgreen Gardens. Their house was build by local laborers, who appreciated the work during the time of the Great Depression. The brick structure was erected without detailed plans but did take into account the potential for hurricanes. A great courtyard with a tower in the center and rooms built as studios for Mrs. Huntington, a sculptress, are unique attributes that make this place worthy of a visit, whether you take a ranger-guided tour or see the facilities on your own. It was last used by the Huntingtons in 1947 and later leased to the State of South Carolina for a park.

What to Do

Relaxing and playing on the beach are obvious attractions at this Atlantic Ocean getaway. Three miles of beachfront attract ocean enthusiasts who go shelling, fish the surf, or just listen to the waves roll in. But Huntington Beach has some other features. Visitors from up north like to see the alligators that repose in the lagoon back from the beach. You can learn more about these ancient creatures from park rangers, for the Huntington Beach State Park education center offers a myriad of naturalist programs about alligators and many other things. Learn about birding, the salt marsh, seashells, whales, and dolphins and take a tour of the historic homesite Atalaya. A jetty at the north end of the park is popular for fishing; surf fishing is good option on the extended beach. Walk the Sandpiper Pond Nature Trail or the Kerrigan Nature Trail. Paddlers can kayak the saltwater marsh toward the mainland. No matter what you do, be glad that the Huntingtons made this getaway available for us all.

What's Nearby

Brookgreen Gardens, founded by the Huntingtons, is across US 17 from the state park. Its 9,000 acres preserve the flora and fauna of the area as well as displaying sculpture pieces. Upon admission you can tour the gardens, enjoy the more than nine hundred sculptures scattered throughout the grounds, see the zoo, or go on a trekker tour. Take a boat trip on the Waccamaw River to view the historic rice plantations of old and perhaps catch a glimpse of alligators, birds, and other wildlife. Special events take place throughout the year. For more information, see www.brookgreen.org.

Information

Huntington Beach State Park
16148 Ocean Highway
Murrells Inlet, SC 29576
(843) 237-4440, www.southcarolinaparks.com; reservations (866) 345-PARK, www.southcarolinaparks.com
Open: Year-round
Sites: 24 water, electric, and sewer sites; 103 water and electric sites; 6 walk-in tent sites
Amenities: Picnic table, water, electricity, some also have sewer; walk-in tent sites have picnic table and fire ring
Registration: By phone, Internet, or at park entrance booth
Facilities: Hot showers, flush toilets, water spigots
Fees: Water, electricity, and sewer sites $21–28; water and electricity sites $20–25; walk-in tent sites $14–19; the higher rates are in summer and at weekends.
Directions: From Myrtle Beach, take US 17 south for 16 miles to the state park, on your left.

Edisto Beach State Park

Edisto Beach, South Carolina

A trip to Edisto Beach State Park is like a trip back in time. This is a quaint park next to a small vacation village with no high-rises and few chain stores. Edisto Beach has been dubbed "Mayberry by the Sea" by those in the know. This South Carolina coastal getaway between Charleston and Savannah, Georgia, should take such a moniker with pride, as it contrasts mightily with other more crowded destinations that have been homogenized by today's proliferation of chain hotels, motels, beach stores, and restaurants. Twenty miles off South Carolina's coastal main drag, US 17, Edisto Beach is at the end of the road. Other easier-to-reach destinations keep it less populated. However, that doesn't make Edisto Beach unpopular. This park and community are what I call a place of return. Families who come here often return year after year and bring their kids, who in turn bring their kids. After you visit to Mayberry by the Sea, you may become a returnee yourself.

Figure 34. Palm trees stand guard at Edisto Beach State Park.

The Beach/Coast

Edisto Beach is on the northern tip of St. Helena Sound, a large bay where the Ashepoo, Combahee, and Edisto rivers converge to meet the Atlantic Ocean. Being an island that directly fronts the Atlantic allows beach formation on Edisto Island, and beaches are what draw people in. Edisto Beach State Park has 1.25 miles of beachfront. The beaches are average in width and allow plenty of sunbathers and beachcombers to roam around. The sandy stretch extends north from the point where the town and the park meet. This park beach is backed by low dunes at the park entrance, with picnic areas shaded by palms and oaks behind the beach. Picnic shelters are also available for hot or rainy days. The park office and gift shop are nearby. Farther down the beach, dunes held by sea oats give way to wind-sculpted maritime brushy vegetation atop the dunes. The Edisto Beach State Park campground lies behind these dunes but is connected to the beach at five access points. The park land ends and private property begins at Edingsville Beach. The village of Edisto Beach stretches south of the park. The ocean here is mostly fronted by houses, but there are numerous public beach accesses along the five miles of beachfront before the land gives way and the island ends at St. Helena Sound.

The Campground

Edisto Beach has two camping areas offering different atmospheres. The Main Camping Area is the more popular, just a dune away from the Atlantic Ocean, with a creek on the mainland side of the campground. The first sites, #1–#12, are among the best. They are spread far apart and are banked against tall dunes. Live oaks shade many of these sites. The road curves away from the beach, then makes a loop in more open terrain at campsites #16–#48. Grass forms the understory for these larger pull-in sites that RVers prefer. The pull-ins are gravel and not leveled. Starting with #32, the campsites overlook the marshy creek away from the beach. Beyond campsite #48, sites are set on both sides of the road and are sporadically shaded by cedars.

The Live Oak Camping Area is less popular simply because it is farther from the beach; you drive to the ocean. It has 50 shaded campsites beneath live oaks and five walk-in tent campsites. These sites are generally larger and more widely separated from one another. Solitude seekers camp back here. The walk-in tent sites are even more remote and very shady. They overlook the marshes of Scott Creek.

The campground can fill at any time during the summer, and reservations are highly recommended from June through August. The campground also sees an upsurge in business during spring break, but since alcohol is not allowed, a family atmosphere reigns throughout the year. This is part of the reason families return year after year.

Human and Natural History

The shortnose sturgeon is an interesting fish that inhabits the tidal rivers of South Carolina. Sturgeon are ancient fish that indeed have a primeval look. They are best known as a source of caviar, and this has led to their being threatened. The shortnose sturgeon is small by sturgeon standards but still can reach nearly five feet in length. The species is found from the lower Canadian Atlantic Coast to northern Florida. In this area, sturgeon ply the areas where fresh and salt water meet. Sturgeon can live more than fifty years and typically grow very slowly. A female sturgeon can produce over 200,000 eggs and can carry an egg mass of over a million eggs, depending on her body size. South Carolina once allowed sturgeon harvesting, but it was shut down in 1985 following precipitous declines in numbers landed in the early 1980s.

What to Do

The original park facilities were developed by the Civilian Conservation Corp in the 1930s. But the number one attraction, the beach, was of course already there and remains the primary draw of this park. Edisto Beach offers a chance to experience the quieter side of the South Carolina coast. Families come here to relax by the ocean and then go back to relax at the campsite. In a place like this, you don't feel compelled to do anything. Some campers surf fish in the Atlantic, while others try the backcountry by boat, using the park boat ramp. Common catches are red drum, trout, and flounder. Paddlers may take out a canoe or sea kayak from this same launch on Big Bay Creek. Charter fishing operations are available in the town of Edisto Beach. Daily interpretive programs are held at the park during the summer. If you prefer to strike out on your own, take a walk on the 3.5-mile Spanish Mount Trail, which travels through the rich woods back from the ocean.

What's Nearby

Edisto Beach State Park is nearly surrounded by the ACE Basin National Estuarine Research Reserve, one of the largest preserved estuaries on the East Coast at 135,000 acres. It is named for the Ashepoo, Combahee, and Edisto rivers, which drain the Low Country west of Edisto Island. The ACE Basin National Estuarine Research Reserve protects the area's beauty, nature's creatures, and the cultural history of the area. In addition, the reserve preserves habitat for many endangered or threatened species, such as the shortnose sturgeon, wood storks, loggerhead sea turtles, and bald eagles. Scientists research the life of the basin and provide important information for those charged with stewardship of our coastlines. The Edisto Interpretive Center, run by ACE Basin, is located off Palmetto Road, near the park boat launch.

Information

Edisto Beach State Park
8377 State Cabin Road
Edisto Island, SC 29438
(843) 869-2756, www.southcarolinaparks.com; reservations (866) 345-PARK, www.southcarolinaparks.com
Open: Year-round
Sites: 113 water and electric sites, 5 walk-in tent sites
Amenities: Picnic table, water, electricity; some also have fire ring
Registration: By phone, Internet, or at park entrance booth
Facilities: Hot showers, flush toilets, pay phone
Fees: Water and electric sites $27 per night Sunday–Thursday, $29 Friday–Saturday; walk-in tent sites $18 per night Sunday–Thursday, $21 Friday–Saturday; off-season rates are lower.
Directions: From Charleston, South Carolina, head south on US 17 for 20 miles to SC 174. Turn left to go south on SC 174 and follow it for 21.7 miles to the state park, on your left.

Myrtle Beach State Park
Myrtle Beach, South Carolina

Myrtle Beach State Park was South Carolina's first state park. When it opened in 1935, the Grand Strand, the tourist Mecca of South Carolina, did not exist. But Myrtle Beach grew as a tourist destination and the Grand Strand expanded to encircle the state park. The park remained, becoming an institution among generations of families visiting year after year to enjoy the natural haven of a coastal preserve with beautiful grounds at the south end of the Grand Strand. Leave the busy strip of vacationer locales and enter a rich forest that contrasts completely with the rest of the townscape. A quiet road leads away from US 17 and into the park. Here is a substantial beach with an even larger campground that defies the stereotypes of such campgrounds. Shady and well cared for, the park makes the most of its natural attributes as the biggest parcel of maritime forest remaining in the greater Myrtle Beach area. You can camp on the coast yet easily reach all the tourist places that Myrtle Beach offers.

The Beach/Coast

High-rises and houses line the shore in this part of South Carolina except at one place, and that is Myrtle Beach State Park. A mile of beachfront is

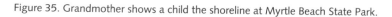

Figure 35. Grandmother shows a child the shoreline at Myrtle Beach State Park.

protected here. The wide beach gently rolls from dunes covered in sea oats down to the Atlantic Ocean. As you pull into the park, you reach the ocean at the park's snack bar and gift shop, which are in the center of the beach area. In the distance the park fishing pier extends far into the water. The pier and park store are attached, so anglers can make those emergency bait and beverage runs. Away from the beach a large picnic area in a mix of shade and sun catches the ocean breezes; the sculpted shapes of the oaks reflect their perpetual exposure to sea breezes.

More beachfront lies south of the fishing pier. Four wooden walkways connect the beach to parking areas. Freshwater showers are available at all the walkways, and picnic tables and covered shelters are adjacent to the parking areas. North of the fishing pier are more picnic and parking areas, and beyond these, a grassy lawn rises up the hill where the former park swimming pools were. A wide trail leads from the campground to the beach, with the park boundary just beyond.

The Campground

This campground is very large, which can be a red flag. But although the immediate area can be bustling, especially on summer weekends, this place does well with its more than 300 campsites. The setting is attractive. Like the rest of the park, the campground is wooded. Tall oaks and pines provide more than ample shade for hot summer days. The campsites are laid out in concentric loops, becoming ever wider, with the exception of a row of sites behind the dune line running parallel to the beach. The campground trading post is in the center of the concentric loops. A laundromat, playground, and bathhouses are also here. The loop roads and campsite pull-ins are gravel, so RVers may have to do a little leveling of their rigs. Circle 1 has some of the largest sites and is closest to the trading post. Circles 2 and 3 have smaller sites. Circle 4 is near the park nature center; Circle 5 is the largest; and Circle 6, with sites #293–#335, has the best sites. These were added later, are a little larger, and lie at the outside of the camping area. Many sites are divided by low vegetation, adding campsite privacy. Circle 6 does have a drawback: it is the farthest from the beach.

The overflow area, with 45 campsites, is close to the park pier and is open only in summer. The sites do not have water or electricity. There is a bathhouse here, and several bathhouses are scattered throughout the main campground. This park fills on weekends from mid-May through August. Sites can be had during the week, but the park does fill on occasion. Reservations are strongly recommended any time in the summer.

Human and Natural History

As the Great Depression deepened in the early 1930s, President Roosevelt came up with the New Deal, and the Civilian Conservation Corps (CCC) was born. The men of the CCC were instrumental in developing Myrtle Beach State Park as well as many other state and national parks throughout the country. For their labor the men received housing, meals, and thirty dollars a month. This gave rise to the saying "another day, another dollar." The Civilian Conservation Corps performed various other kinds of work throughout South Carolina, including soil conservation, reforestation, and fire prevention besides the development of recreational areas. Thanks to the CCC, Myrtle Beach State Park opened in July 1936 and the South Carolina state park system was born. By 1938, fourteen South Carolina state parks were open. The CCC was disbanded in 1942, due to World War II. However, by then South Carolina had opened even more state parks. Today the Palmetto State has forty-seven state parks ready for your visit.

What to Do

Primary park activities center on the ocean. The facilities here are designed to handle a lot of visitors. The park beach can get crowded with shoreline lovers engaging in every type of pastime. The fishing pier draws in fishermen galore going after whiting, Spanish mackerel, flounder, and sea trout, among other fish. Limited park size limits park activities largely to camping and beach happenings, though nature trails do wind through the maritime forest if you are looking for a break from the sun. The park has daily interpretive programs during the summer, many of them based out of the park nature center, which is adjacent to the campground.

What's Nearby

Proximity means many people enjoy the attractions at nearby tourist destinations in Myrtle Beach, ranging from miniature golf and waterslides to dinner shows. The area claims to receive over 14 million visitors per year to local attractions and the 60 miles of beaches along the Grand Strand. Just inland of those beaches are tourist pursuits of every stripe: shopping, amusement parks, go-kart rides, and eateries line US 17. It's a fun place for people watching. Shoppers may be looking for the perfect grass basket from the area or a hammock from nearby Pawleys Island. Myrtle Beach State Park fits the bill whether you prefer to shop, play on the beach, or enjoy the protected acreage of the park.

Information

Myrtle Beach State Park
4401 South Kings Highway
Myrtle Beach, SC 29575
(843) 238-5325, www.southcarolinaparks.com; reservations (866) 345-PARK, www.southcarolinaparks.com
Open: Year-round
Sites: 302 water and electric sites; 45 overflow primitive sites open June–August
Amenities: Hot showers, flush toilets, laundry, camp store, pay phone
Registration: By phone, Internet, or at park entrance booth
Facilities: Hot showers, flush toilets, laundry, camp store
Fees: Standard sites $23–25 per night; overflow tent sites, $17–19; off-season rates are lower
Directions: From the city of Myrtle Beach head south on US 17 Business for 3 miles. The park is on your left, a little south of the entrance to Myrtle Beach Airport.

North Carolina

Carolina Beach State Park
Carolina Beach, North Carolina

Carolina Beach State Park is your headquarters for exploring the southeastern coast of North Carolina. The park itself is a fine destination with a shady campground, hiking trails, and access to the Intracoastal Waterway. It is home to one of America's most unusual plants, the Venus flytrap, which traps and consumes insects—more about the flytrap later.

Take note that the park does not have direct beach access. However, Fort Fisher State Recreation Area just a short distance away offers seven miles of beachfront on the Atlantic Ocean. This is also the locale of historic Fort Fisher, a Civil War fort you can tour. In addition the North Carolina Aquarium is just down the road, and the historic town of Wilmington, North Carolina, is up the road, further enhancing Carolina Beach as a great base camp for exploring this segment of the Atlantic Coast.

The Beach/Coast

Carolina Beach State Park is bordered on two sides by water. Snows Cut is on the north and is part of the Intracoastal Waterway. Visitors can access the waterway by foot trail only. On the west the wide Cape Fear River extends beyond the land. The park has a marina located near where Snows Cut meets the Cape Fear River. A fishing deck is available for park visitors near the marina. The Sugarloaf Trail runs along the Cape Fear River. No swimming is allowed in the park, but there is no need for this with Fort Fisher State Recreation Area a few miles to the south on US 421.

A boardwalk connects the beach at Fort Fisher to the visitor center, which has outside showers and restrooms. Once you reach the beach you have seven miles of undeveloped shoreline to enjoy. Lifeguards are present in summer from Memorial Day to Labor Day. Vehicles are allowed on the beach south of the visitor center beach area, though they must stay on a designated route. The towns of Carolina Beach at Pleasant Island and Kure Beach also have public beach access if you prefer to stay closer to the campground.

The Campground

Carolina Beach campground is set amid pines near Snows Cut. The evergreens stand tall over the two campground loops. Live oaks, water oaks, and other hardwoods are mixed in with the pines. Clumpy brush grows here and there among the woods, adding privacy, especially on the second loop. Sunlight filters through the tall trees. A drive on the paved campground road through the first loop, with sites #1–#47, shows big campsites with a sand and pine needle floor. The pull-ins are not paved, and some may require leveling for big rigs. RVers need to be apprised that there is no water or electricity at the campsites. A short road with large campsites along it leads to the second loop, and a bathhouse centers each loop.

The second loop has campsite sites #48–#82, also large but more secluded, and it may be closed during quiet times. The sites in the second loop are used less, but the first loop doesn't get a whole lot of business itself. This park has an unusual system of obtaining campsites. A little green tag hangs below each numbered campsite post. When you find a site you like, grab the green tag and take it to the park store and marina, then register there. The campground fills during most weekends from Memorial Day through the Fourth of July. After that, the heat keeps most campers away until fall, when the park grows busy during weekends of ideal weather, but usually not full. A campsite can be had most spring weekends and any time during winter. With no reservations allowed you are always taking a chance, but a chance to come here is worth it.

Human and Natural History

Visitors come to this area for the beaches, but don't forget about the plant with the catchy name, the unusual Venus flytrap. The modified leaves of this plant close rapidly when an insect touches tiny hairs on the inside of the plant, trapping the insect, which is then ingested by the Venus flytrap. The nutrition provided by the insects supplements what the plants can extract from the poor, sandy soils of the area. This unusual plant grows only on land located within a 60-mile radius of Wilmington, North Carolina, ocean areas excepted. The Fly Trap Trail in Carolina Beach State Park leads past stands of the plants in their natural surroundings.

What to Do

Besides the Fly Trap Trail the park has several other hiking trails crisscrossing numerous natural communities. The Sugarloaf Trail passes through tidal flat and pine woods. The Snows Cut Trail leads to the Intracoastal Waterway. The Swamp Trail is self-explanatory, and the Campground Trail connects your camp to the rest of the trail network. These six miles of trails are mostly hiked during cooler times. As noted, a fishing deck leading into the Cape Fear River is located near the park marina. Fishermen go for croaker, flounder, and striped bass. The marina sells plenty of bait and tackle. You can enjoy the convenience of the boat launch at the marina. Fort Fisher State Recreation Area is your best bet for oceanic endeavors, with its miles of beachfront to explore and enjoy. It also has a hiking trail of its own, the Basin Trail, which leads to an overlook. And don't forget about the closer beach access points in Carolina Beach.

What's Nearby

Located just across the road from Fort Fisher State Recreation Area is the state historic site of the fort itself, scene of the largest remaining earthworks in the South. You can visit the fort museum and enjoy the guided tours that allow you to walk the earthworks.

During the Civil War Fort Fisher was the location of the largest land-sea battle fought in any war in history. In early 1865, a fleet of fifty-six ships bombarded the fort prior to a land assault by a force of more than thirty-three hundred infantry. Fort Fisher was captured and the Confederate supply line was broken. The fall of Fort Fisher was one of the last nails in the coffin for the Confederacy; the war ended three months after Fort Fisher changed hands.

Information

Carolina Beach State Park
P.O. Box 475
Carolina Beach, NC 28428
(910) 458-8206, www.ils.unc.edu/parkproject/ncparks.html
Open: Year-round
Sites: 83
Amenities: Picnic table, grill
Registration: At park marina office
Facilities: Hot showers, flush toilets, water spigots, camp store
Fees: $15 per night
Directions: From Wilmington, drive south on US 421 for 15 miles, crossing the Intracoastal Waterway. Turn right on Dow Road past the Intracoastal Waterway, shortly reaching the park on your right.

Ocracoke Island, Cape Hatteras National Seashore
Ocracoke, North Carolina

Ocracoke Island is the southernmost place at Cape Hatteras National Seashore. You can only reach the 17-mile-long barrier island by airplane or ferry. Vehicle ferries run between Ocracoke and Cape Hatteras, and it can also be reached by ferry from two mainland sites. Smart campers will have made reservations for the National Park Service campground on the island. Once on the ferry your troubles will melt away and you can shift into "island time."

And Ocracoke is no ordinary island. Its slow-moving traffic, narrow streets, and lack of franchise operations are a refreshing change from ordinary life. The island has played a significant role in American sea history, both as headquarters for pirates—notably Blackbeard himself—and later as a wreck salvaging center. Being a barrier island, Ocracoke has miles and miles of Atlantic beachfront to explore. And it has its own lighthouse, which shines on a funky ocean village that makes a great place for a beach vacation.

Figure 36. The Ocracoke Island Lighthouse was completed in 1823.

The Beach/Coast

Ocracoke Island is a segment of the greater Cape Hatteras National Seashore. The island has a good mix of public and private land, allowing more than ample beach access close to facilities such as stores, restaurants, and tourist getaways that private operations can offer. The narrow Ocracoke Island runs on a southwest-northeast axis. Its widest part is where the village of Ocracoke stands. Pamlico Sound divides the island from the mainland, which is a long distance away. The Atlantic Ocean fronts the south side of the island and offers more beach than most of us are willing to walk. The short free ferry from Cape Hatteras reaches the eastern side of Ocracoke, while the two mainland ferries reach the island at Ocracoke village from Swan Quarter and Cedar Island. The eastern half of the Atlantic-facing beach is closed to vehicles year-round and offers getaways for those seeking solitude. The beach is within easy walking distance of the campground and there are two auto ramps nearby for accessing the ocean. The beach between the campground and the village has lifeguards present between Memorial Day and Labor Day. The Banker Pony Pens are located on the north side of NC 12, which runs the length of the island. The most southerly point of the island can be reached in a four-wheel-drive vehicle from South Point Road.

The Campground

The campground is not a great draw in itself. Located in a flat behind dunes that separate you from the beach and the Atlantic Ocean, it is a grassy area punctuated with just a few small cedar and other trees, pruned back by the relentless wind. The paved loop is broken by three crossroads. Campsite pull-ins are paved as well and all are level, making life a little easier for big rigs. However, be apprised that sites have no water or electricity hookups.

The loop curves around to reach the campsites that back up to the sand dunes. These dune sites are open to the sun but larger, and tent campers can find a spot for the tent back from the parking pad; other average sites have tent areas directly by the parking pad. The sites on the inside of the loop are small and pinched in together and are better for self-contained rigs. The loop then curves away from the shore, but even these sites are within an easy walk of the beach. The campsites on the cross-loop roads are mostly flat, grassy, and open to the sun. Three separate bathroom areas with cold showers are spread through the campground.

Being able to make reservations may be the best thing about the camp-ground. Reservations can be made only for the period between mid-May and mid-September; they are highly recommended for holiday weekends and from early July through mid-August. Be aware that mosquitoes can be a prob-lem after wet spells. Mosquito repellent and a screen shelter will make your stay much more enjoyable. Furthermore, if you are taking either the Cedar Island ferry or the Swan Quarter ferry from the mainland, make reservations for your arrival and departure during the busy season. I recommend coming during spring and fall when the crowds are absent.

Human and Natural History

The Ocracoke light is the second oldest operating lighthouse in the nation. It was finished in 1823. The lighthouse stands 75 feet tall, its diameter narrow-ing from 25 feet at the base to 12 feet at its peak. The walls are solid brick—12 feet thick at the bottom tapering to two feet at the top. An octagonal lantern crowns the tower and houses the light beacon. The exterior's solid white color serves as its identifying mark to mariners by day. The original whitewash rec-ipe called for blending lime, salt, Spanish whiting, rice, glue, and boiling wa-ter. The mixture was applied while still hot. Today, paint is used. Originally an oil-burning light, the Ocracoke Light was electrified in the early 1900s. The light can be seen from 14 miles out at sea. The lighthouse keeper's quarters still stand on the site today. You can visit the lighthouse grounds but climbing the structure is not allowed.

What to Do

As I have hinted already, the clocks at Ocracoke are set on island time. Slow yourself down with a walk on the beach. A great place for quiet beachcomb-ing is the beach access area across from the pony pens. No cars are allowed on the beach here, and no development can be seen. Cars are allowed on the beach near the campground. Sea kayaking is popular on the Pamlico Sound side of the island, as is kiteboarding.

The ponies that once roamed Ocracoke are now cared for by the park ser-vice. They are quartered a few miles from the campground, at the Banker Pony Pens. The animals are thought to have swum ashore from a Spanish shipwreck long ago. An interpretive trail travels near the horse pens. Another interpre-tive trail, the Hardwood Hammocks Trail, travels three quarters of a mile into the island interior. The path starts just across the road from the campground. Remember to walk slowly, as everything moves on island time.

What's Nearby

The village of Ocracoke is just a few miles from the campground. If you ride either of the mainland ferries, you will come through Ocracoke before you reach the campground. This place has character, so check it out. Stop at the park visitor center in town for information and enjoy interpretive programs that will help you appreciate the island more. Then walk a few feet and sit back on a bench at Silver Lake Harbor to watch the boats come and go. Take the Ocracoke Historical Interpretive Trail to learn about the lengthy past of this island. Boats of all sorts can be rented in the village of Ocracoke. You can also rent bikes for pedaling around the village, or charter a sport fishing boat. Bring some extra cash and splurge for a restaurant meal. One final note—make a quick visit to photograph the Ocracoke Lighthouse. Parking is limited at the beacon.

Information

Ocracoke Campground, Cape Hatteras National Seashore
Route 1, Box 675
Manteo, NC 27954
(252) 928-4531, www.nps.gov/caha; reservations (800) 365-CAMP; ferry information (800) 293-3779, www.ncferry.org
Open: Late March through mid-October
Sites: 136
Amenities: Picnic table, upright grill
Registration: By phone, Internet, or at park entrance booth
Facilities: Cold showers, flush toilets, water spigots
Fees: $20 per night
Directions: From the intersection of US 64/264 and US 158 just south of Nags Head, drive south on NC 12 for 59 miles to the ferry at the southwest end of Hatteras Island. From here, take the free ferry over to Ocracoke Island. Once off the ferry, keep south on NC 12 for 9.5 miles to reach the campground, on your left. There are two other, longer toll ferry options to reach Ocracoke Island. For more ferry information call (800) 293-3779, or visit www.ncferry.org.

Frisco Campground, Cape Hatteras National Seashore

Frisco, North Carolina

Frisco Campground is located near one of America's most notable oceanside landmarks, the Cape Hatteras Lighthouse—the tallest lighthouse in the United States. The lighthouse was moved in 1999, due to an eroding shoreline not far from where it stands today. This beacon's striped black and white paint job helps it stand out. Today the lighthouse, still operating, is a huge drawing card at Cape Hatteras National Seashore, of which Frisco Campground is a part. Frisco Campground is a draw in its own right, with campsites set amid dunes that are among the highest on the Outer Banks. Campers can duck into the brush in deep swales or camp in the open with dune-top views

Figure 37. Cape Hatteras Lighthouse, near Frisco Campground, is the most famous lighthouse in the United States.

far our over the Atlantic Ocean. Viewing the Cape Hatteras Lighthouse is a must among Frisco campers.

The Beach/Coast

Cape Hatteras is the point where North Carolina's Outer Banks shift from a north-south axis to a northwest-southeast axis. The cape area is arguably the widest part of the Outer Banks and also has its highest ground. This results in some of the richest land diversity on the Outer Banks, culminating in the Buxton Woods, a rich forest on the cape's interior. This curve of land keeps Pamlico Sound, the waterway between the Outer Banks and the mainland, smoother than elsewhere, and keeps the waters south of Frisco among the warmest on the Outer Banks. Miles and miles of beach north and south of the cape are available for exploration. Cape Hatteras Lighthouse attracts visitors who walk up it for a view and to see where it formerly stood. The beach adjacent to the beacon is a popular swimming beach on the Atlantic side. The Pamlico Sound side of the area is private land with houses and stores. Campers can access the beach from Frisco via two boardwalks. However, many visitors drive to the beach, and there is an access ramp at Frisco—four-wheel-drive is required. Nearby Cape Point also has a beach access, and you can head out to the tip of Cape Hatteras. West of the campground are a fishing pier and the Sandy Bay beach access, which has a bathhouse.

The Campground

The campground is laid out in a big loop with six roads crossing over the loop. The roads and pull-ins are paved, eliminating worry about RVs getting stuck. The whole camping area overlies a series of dunes, ever increasing in height as you head away from the ocean. The Atlantic shore runs parallel to the campground and is about 150 yards distant. Scattered cedars, oaks, and pines mostly grow brushy, sculpted by ocean breezes. The tops of dunes have less vegetation. Trees are taller in the swales, but few grow taller than head-high. Nevertheless, campsites with even a modicum of shade are quickly snapped up. Most sites are completely in the open.

The main loop curves around, passing some pine trees in the low area between the campground and the beach, which is accessed by two boardwalks. The road rises and climbs atop high dunes, overlooking the ocean in far-reaching panoramas. Sites here, like the rest, have good and bad points:

open sites are exposed to the wind, which cuts down on mosquitoes, but if the wind is cold, then the openness is a negative. If the sun is blaring down, as it often is, then the lack of shade can be wearing. Bringing a screen shelter can eliminate both sun and bug problems. Many sites are small; tent campers need to be flexible in setting up, whereas RV rigs can just park on the pull-in. Drive around the campground when you arrive—it is first come, first served. Campers usually end up finding a site that feels right. Frisco fills on major holidays and a few other summer weekends of perfect weather.

Human and Natural History

Mariners from days gone by used currents along with wind to travel, and staying within sight of land aided navigation. Both the south-running Labrador Current and the north-running Gulf Stream travel near the Outer Banks, so ships frequently passed by Cape Hatteras. But shifting shoals and weather factors led to numerous ships wrecking here, leading to the area being dubbed the "Graveyard of the Atlantic." Lighthouses were clearly needed to aid navigation. At one time lighthouses were spread approximately 40 miles apart all along the Carolina coast, so that mariners could always keep a beacon within sight. The lighthouses had different light flash patterns, and were painted differently, in order for sailors to distinguish between the beacons. Nobody knows why the Cape Hatteras Lighthouse got its distinctive striped paint job, but it adds to the scenic nature of the light.

What to Do

Of course, a tour of the Cape Hatteras Lighthouse is in order. It is but a short drive from Frisco. There is a fee to climb the lighthouse. In the summer, I suggest climbing the lighthouse in the morning, as it can get hot and stuffy in the afternoon inside the structure. Enjoy the view once atop the lighthouse—you can see for miles. Survey your sand and water domain. Perhaps pick out a place to hit the beach on foot or by vehicle. Four-wheel-drive vehicles can access the beach at many areas of Cape Hatteras National Seashore. The access points are called ramps. A ramp is located adjacent to the campground. Most Frisco campers simply use the boardwalks to reach the beach. In either case, you have miles of shoreline to enjoy, whether you are surf casting or surfing with a board. Another morning activity is to hike the Buxton Woods Trail, which is operated in conjunction with the Nature Conservancy. You can enjoy the cape's most extensive woodland.

What's Nearby

The village of Frisco has supplies and stores and also a few attractions. The Frisco Native American Museum has artifacts from the area Indians, but also all over the country. A nature trail runs behind the museum. Fishing charters are available in Frisco. The interesting town of Ocracoke is worth a visit, and is accessible via ferry west of Frisco campground.

Information

Frisco Campground, Cape Hatteras National Seashore
Route 1, Box 675
Manteo, NC 27954
(252) 995-4474, www.nps.gov/caha
Open: Late March through early October
Sites: 127
Amenities: Picnic table, upright grill
Registration: At park entrance booth
Facilities: Cold showers, flush toilets, water spigots
Fees: $20 per night
Directions: From the intersection of US 64/264 and US 158 just south of Nags Head, drive south on NC 12 for 60 miles to the hamlet of Frisco. Turn left on Billy Mitchell Road and follow it for 1 mile to reach the campground.

Oregon Inlet, Cape Hatteras National Seashore
Nags Head, North Carolina

Location is one of the best attributes of this campground. Oregon Inlet on Bodie Island is the most northerly campground at Cape Hatteras National Seashore, on North Carolina's Outer Banks a few miles south of Nags Head. Consequently a visit offers not only activities at the national seashore but also things to do north of the national seashore, such as seeing some of the area firsts—site of the first airplane flight by the Wright Brothers at Kitty Hawk, and one of the continent's first European settlements at Fort Raleigh, birthplace of Virginia Dare, who was the first person of European descent born on the continent. Oregon Inlet campground lies behind tall dunes and has miles of beach to explore at nearby Coquina Beach and Pea Island National Wildlife Refuge. The national seashore is a place of lighthouses, and Oregon Inlet has one nearby, the Bodie Island Lighthouse. Just remember that location is what Oregon Inlet is all about: the appeal of the area is in the surrounding attractions rather than the campground itself.

Figure 38. Bodie Island Lighthouse is located near Oregon Inlet Campground.

The Beach/Coast

North Carolina's Outer Banks are a narrow swath of ever changing barrier islands, a mix of public and private lands, with the hard-charging Atlantic Ocean to the east and shallow, quieter waters between the Outer Banks and the mainland. Cape Hatteras National Seashore and Pea Island National Wildlife Refuge, just south of Oregon Inlet, allow recreational access to the Outer Banks. The Wright Brothers National Memorial is north of Oregon Inlet. Moving south, you pass Jockey Ridge State Park, which has tall dunes. Then you reach the national seashore at Bodie Island. Parts of Bodie Island are privately owned, but the last 4.5 miles of Atlantic frontage are open to the public. Coquina Beach is a public access point in the national seashore with a bathhouse and outdoor showers connected to the beach by a boardwalk. Parts of the national seashore beachfront are open to vehicles, depending upon the time of the year and the state of the beach. Call ahead if you are interested in taking your vehicle onto the beach. If you wish to avoid cars on the beach, Oregon Inlet has good options. Nearby Coquina Beach is always closed to vehicles. Pea Island National Wildlife Refuge to the south has several access points along its 13 miles of beaches, which are always closed to vehicles. The actual watery Oregon Inlet is a quarter mile away from the Atlantic, separated from it by dunes and not offering direct beach access.

The Campground

The ocean is not visible from the Oregon Inlet campground because of the high dunes. There are no trees and hence the campground has no shade; the only vegetation consists of small shrubs, sea oats, and grass between the sites. The sites do not have water or power hookups. The 120 mostly level sites are situated in three loops. Loop A curves left away from the entrance station. The first sites are banked against the dunes. Like the other loops, Loop A has a paved road and paved pull-ins that keep big rigs level. Tent campers need to know that tent pads are not available and dune sites have little level ground on which to set your tent. Screen shelters are recommended to provide shade and refuge from insects, which can be troublesome after rainy periods.

The first several sites on Loop B bank against the dunes. This can be helpful if the weather is cold or windy. Tent and screen shelter spots are limited. However, open sites can be desirable for their insect-ridding breezes. The sites away from the dunes are more open and offer grassy spots to put up a tent.

Loop C has entirely level sites and is most popular with the big rigs. Tent campers form the majority in summer, but hard-sided campers predominate in spring and fall. Oregon Inlet is a first come, first served campground. It fills on summer holiday weekends and weekends of nice weather from June through August. Sites are almost always available during the week. Bathhouses with cold showers are available, as are water spigots.

Human and Natural History

Bodie Island was proposed as a lighthouse location for mariners to orient themselves before working around Cape Hatteras. Bodie Island, north of the cape, was a location of many shipwrecks, especially by southbound boats. The first lighthouse went up in 1847, but it was built on a poor foundation and began to lean before being abandoned in 1859. A second lighthouse was built, but it was blown up by the Confederates to deter Union usage as an observation post. A decade later the third lighthouse, the one we see today, was erected. The oil-based light needed a full-time keeper until it was electrified in 1932. Today, the 156-foot structure is set to be restored inside and out. Campers at Oregon Inlet may in due course be able to climb this tower just as people climb the more famous Cape Hatteras Lighthouse.

What to Do

Being near the edge of the national seashore means campers at Oregon Inlet can enjoy activities both inside and outside the conserved area. As noted, the beaches at Coquina Beach and the Pea Island National Wildlife Refuge are close, and campers can engage in all manner of beach activities from surf fishing and surfing to building sand castles or just sitting underneath the umbrella, slowing down life's fast pace, and watching other people have fun. If you take your fishing more seriously a fishing center is just across NC 12 from the campground. A store offers tackle and other supplies. Fishing charters can be had here as well. Campers at Oregon Inlet like to come over to the fishing center in the afternoon to survey the catches of the day on the charters.

The Bodie Island Visitor Center is nearby. Here you can check out the historic Bodie Island Lighthouse and the adjacent buildings, including the light keeper's quarters, which now house interpretive information about the area and a small book store. Daily interpretive programs are conducted out of the visitor center and take place there or at Coquina Beach. North of the seashore, visitors can see Fort Raleigh National Historic Site, the location of the first European-originated colony in North Carolina. The memorial to the Wright Brothers at the place where people first took flight is a short drive away (see following section). Flight of the natural variety is a focus at Pea Island to the south, where birders enjoy the avian viewing as well as the beaches.

What's Nearby

A must for anyone visiting the area is the Wright Brothers National Memorial. This site, run by the National Park Service, is located in the hills north of the national seashore. The Wright Brothers Monument atop Kill Devil Hill is a 60-foot granite marker honoring the Ohio siblings who were the first to fly an airplane successfully. Just north of the monument you can see the exact spot where the first flights took place and the camp where the brothers stayed as they attempted their historic feat. They chose the area because of its tall dunes, high winds, and sand for softer landings. The Wright Brothers National Memorial is located north of Nags Head on NC 12.

Information

Oregon Inlet, Cape Hatteras National Seashore
Route 1, Box 675
Manteo, NC 27954
(252) 441-5711, www.nps.gov/caha
Open: Late March through early October
Sites: 120
Amenities: Picnic table, upright grill
Registration: At campground entrance station
Facilities: Cold showers, flush toilets, water spigots
Fees: $20 per night
Directions: From the intersection of US 64/264 and US 158 just south of Nags Head drive south on NC 12 for 9 miles to the campground, on your left.

Virginia

First Landing State Park
Virginia Beach, Virginia

This park was formerly known as Seashore State Park. True to its former name, the park stands sentinel on the south cape of the opening to Chesapeake Bay, known as Cape Henry, on the seashore where the bay meets the Atlantic Ocean. To some old-time visitors it will always be known as Seashore State Park. But the newer moniker recognizes its place as the site of the first landing of the English colonizers who later landed at Jamestown. Name aside, it remains Virginia's most popular state park. And why not, with its beach frontage overlooking the entrance to Chesapeake Bay?

Figure 39. First Landing State Park at sunrise.

The park also has an elaborate trail system on the landward side. The campground is in an interesting and attractive setting amid dunes that give way to a scenic maritime live oak hammock. Originally developed by the Civilian Conservation Corps in the 1930s, this park that was once in a quiet area is now surrounded by urban development, but it remains an outpost of nature for enjoyment and recreation.

The Beach/Coast

The park once covered the entire area of Cape Henry, the curve of land extending into Chesapeake Bay. However, during World War II the outermost part of the cape was commandeered by the military and was turned into Fort Story, a defensive garrison. Later the fort evolved into the training station that it is today. The old Cape Henry Lighthouse is still here, as are the Cape Henry National Memorial and the new Cape Henry Lighthouse. The hotel- and tourist-establishment-lined Virginia Beach runs south of Cape Henry and is a fun place if you want to delve into the busier side of beach life. The park beach begins west of Fort Story. It has 1.25 miles of beachfront looking out on Chesapeake Bay. A surprisingly wide sand beach gives way to sea oats–covered dunes that rise to 75 feet, the highest point in the far east of Virginia. Two beach access boardwalks cross the dunes and allow beachcombers and others to enjoy this pretty locale where ships pass with regularity in the distance. More high-rises extend west of the park boundaries, as does the Chesapeake Bay Bridge and Tunnel crossing Chesapeake Bay.

The Campground

The campground features a real mix of sites, most of them good. It is busy and shows a little wear and tear but has received a facelift, with water and electricity being added to many sites as well as the bathhouses being fixed up. The camping area is strung out parallel to Chesapeake Bay and US 60; road noise is audible from the sites away from the bay. The campground sits on a series of wooded dunes that offer hills and vertical variation. The dunes are sandier near the bay and become less sandy and more wooded the farther you get from the bay. Beautiful wind-sculpted oak trees and miniature cypress swamps add scenic variety to the camping area. Understory brush separates many sites. The sites closest to the bay are the most popular; they have less vegetation for shade but get better breezes.

The campground fills daily in summer. Reservations are highly recommended. Make sure to indicate what kind of camping you will be doing—RV or tent—and the staff will do their best to accommodate you. Given the mix of sizes and types of campsites, once you come here in person you will find a site to your liking and then return to it in the future. Spring and fall are good times to come; the campground is a lot less busy.

Human and Natural History

The First Landing that gave the park its name occurred on April 26, 1607. English colonists of the Virginia Company of London had sailed for four months across the Atlantic Ocean. Upon seeing land they just had to stop, though their orders were to establish their colony farther inland. They got just inside Chesapeake Bay, anchored up, and headed ashore. The colonists wandered this very area, though the shift of land over four hundred years has left the exact spot lost to time. They saw tall trees and flowing fresh water (a real treat after the long voyage) and a beautiful Virginia spring coming alive. Before they left, they also had a little run-in with the local Indians, who wounded two Englishmen.

The next day they went ashore again and built a boat to explore the lower Chesapeake Bay. The English enjoyed the beauty and potential of what they named Cape Henry but kept pushing inland, up what is now called the James River to Jamestown and the first permanent English settlement in the Americas.

What to Do

The waters of Chesapeake Bay and the beaches along its shore are popular draws. Boardwalks lead from the campground directly to the beach, where people swim and enjoy the surf. Others relax beneath umbrellas and watch the massive ships plying the bay. If you have your own boat, the park has a launch at the south end in an area known as The Narrows.

A special feature of this park is its commingling of southern and northern flora and fauna. This is such a biologically rich area that it was named a National Natural Landmark in 1965. You can explore its riches on its major trail system of 19 miles, a network that draws locals for day use. The most popular segment is the Bald Cypress Trail, which rings a dark cypress swamp. The Osmanthus Trail is longer at 3.1 miles. The Cape Henry Trail is 6 miles long and is open to bikers and hikers. The Long Creek Trail roughly follows Broad Bay. You will have to find out about the rest of the trail system yourself.

What's Nearby

The oceanside portion of the town of Virginia Beach is just a few miles distant. You can get into just about anything there. Atlantic Avenue is great for people watching and dining. The Cape Henry National Monument is on a property that offers three interesting sights: the old Cape Henry Lighthouse—the first beacon to be commissioned by the United States, first lit in 1792; the new Cape Henry Lighthouse; and the Cape Henry National Monument itself, honoring those who were part of the First Landing. All three are on Fort Story Military Reservation, so expect to be stopped due to Homeland Security requirements. Make sure and go in at Gate 1 at Fort Story to see these sights.

Information

First Landing State Park
2500 Shore Drive
Virginia Beach, VA 23451-1415
(757) 412-2300, www.dcr.state.va.us/parks; reservations (800) 933-PARK, www.dcr.state.va.us/parks
Open: March through November
Sites: 76 electric and water sites, 89 standard sites
Amenities: Hot showers, flush toilets, laundry, camp store
Registration: By phone, Internet, or at park entrance booth
Facilities: Hot showers, flush toilets, pay phone
Fees: Sites with water and electricity $28 per night; standard sites $22 per night
Directions: From exit 282 on I-64 in Norfolk, take Northampton Boulevard/US 13 north. Follow it to the last exit before the Chesapeake Bay Bridge and Tunnel, which is Shore Drive/US 60. Turn right on Shore Drive/US 60 and follow it for 4.5 miles to the campground entrance of the park, on your left.

Kiptopeke State Park

Kiptopeke, Virginia

The site of Kiptopeke State Park, just inside Chesapeake Bay, has undergone many a change through the years. The bay portion of the park was originally purchased by the State of Virginia as a ferry landing for passengers between Virginia Beach and the Eastern Shore, as this part of the Delmarva Peninsula is known. The name Eastern Shore comes from the peninsula forming the eastern shoreline of Chesapeake Bay. Over time, the ferry landing of the Eastern Shore was moved. Later, a private operator developed a campground near the old ferry landing. In 1992 the state purchased the private campground and developed day use facilities at the former ferry landing. The plan has worked well, resulting in a fine state park that offers a good camping area, quality beach and bay access, and a few other surprises, such as being a major birding locale on the Eastern Flyway. All this adds up to a great place to spend a few days along Virginia's Eastern Shore.

Figure 40. Parts of the beach at Kiptopeke are preserved as natural areas.

The Beach/Coast

Kiptopeke features a little over a mile of bayfront. High bluffs drop down to rolling wooded dunes and then to a sandy beach overlooking Chesapeake Bay. The center of the bayfront is a developed area. Old concrete ships from World War II are located about 150 yards offshore as a breakwater. The breakwater function dates from the days of the ferries, but today the old ships act as fish attractors and are instrumental in the deposition of sand for the beach here. A boat launch allows access to the bay. A large and long L-shaped fishing pier extends into the water from a parking area.

This developed area divides the park beaches. The North Beach begins near the boat ramp and curves north for a half mile before giving way to tall bluffs. A swimming beach, with lifeguards in the summer, is here. Farther up, two long and elaborate boardwalks reach down from the park campground over old dunes to the North Beach. A bathhouse is conveniently located near the swimming beach. This area is where families gather. The South Beach is better for beachcombing. It also has two boardwalk accesses. The beach curves to reach the park natural area and recently acquired additional park acreage. The last part of the beach is off limits as it is a protected natural area.

The Campground

The park campground is a fine destination for both tent and RV campers. The grounds are well maintained by park staff and camp hosts. The campground is divided into two areas, putting likeminded RV campers together and tent campers together. The RV area is in the front. It has sites with electric, water, and sewer hookups. The pull-ins are not paved, however, so you may have to do a little leveling. Even-numbered campsites #2–#42 are your best bet. These are partially shaded by tall pines. The next sites are mostly open to the sun overhead and are laid out in long rows, separated by grass. RVs naturally congregate here, with the utility hookups.

The tent sites are divided into three loops set in shady pine woods mixed with hardwoods. They do not have water or electricity and are cheaper. These sites are good for a hot summer day. The loop with sites #122–#141 is closest to the beach walkways. Two large bathhouses serve the campground. Reservations are highly recommended at Kiptopeke during the summer. From Memorial Day through Labor Day the park is full every weekend and on some weekdays in nice weather. The park also rents on-site travel trailers and has a unique camping yurt located on a bluff above the bay. The yurt could be described as a permanent round tent. The travel trailers allow you to experience hard-sided camping. Contact the park for further details about these camping options.

Human and Natural History

Chesapeake Bay is one of the richest estuaries in the world. It has 2,500 square miles of water bordered by 4,000 miles of shoreline. One of its most common inhabitants is the blue crab. The crab itself isn't blue, but the pincers of adult male crabs are blue. Over its two- to three-year life span, the crab sheds its shell more than twenty times. This is known as molting. The stages of the molting process have given rise to different names for the blue crab, depending on its shell stage. For example, a buster is a crab with a shell that has split. A peeler is a crab that is losing its shell. A softshell crab has just lost its shell. The papershell crab's shell is just beginning to harden, and its shell is thin, like paper. Blue crabs migrate up the bay in spring and down the bay in fall. Chesapeake Bay yields millions of crabs per year from its waters.

What to Do

The beach is a big draw, especially in summer when lifeguards are present. This beach, bordered by high bluffs, is especially scenic. The concrete sunken ships keep the waters from becoming too rough. Fishing is big here, whether you utilize the park pier or launch your own boat. Anglers go for black drum, reds, croaker, and sea trout. The fishing pier has 1,000 feet of space and is lighted at night to attract fish.

Kiptopeke is an important birding area. It is on the Eastern Flyway and birders crowd the park in September and October. There is a bird banding station that has been in operation since 1963. You can also enjoy the interface between woodland and water on the four miles of park trails. They combine boardwalks with standard footpaths. The trails emanate from the park picnic area, which has two picnic shelters and a playground for kids. The park also offers naturalist programs during the summer and birding-specific programs in September and October.

What's Nearby

Eastern Shore National Wildlife Refuge is just a short drive from Kiptopeke State Park. Virginia's Eastern Shore, a long narrow spit of land surrounded by water, acts as a funnel for bird migration. In fall, literally millions of birds gather in this area at the southern tip of the Delmarva Peninsula, waiting for favorable wind and weather conditions before undertaking the crossing of Chesapeake Bay. Stop at the refuge visitor center and get the lie of the land, then head out on a couple of nature trails or take the Fisherman's Island tour, which is offered fall through spring. This is the only way to get onto this protected parcel of land.

Information

Kiptopeke State Park
3540 Kiptopeke Drive
Cape Charles, VA 23310
(757) 331-2267, www.dcr.state.va.us/parks; reservations (800) 933-PARK, www.dcr.state.va.us/parks
Open: March through November
Sites: 94 electric, water, and sewer sites; 46 standard sites
Amenities: Electricity, water, sewer, fire ring, picnic table in sites #1–#94; rest of sites have picnic table and fire ring
Registration: By phone, Internet, or at park entrance booth
Facilities: Hot showers, flush toilets, laundry, camp store
Fees: Sites with electricity, water, and sewer $31 per night; sites with electricity and water $28 per night; standard sites $22 per night
Directions: From Virginia Beach drive north on US 13 across the Chesapeake Bay Bridge and Tunnel. After leaving the bridge, continue for three miles to VA 704. Turn left on VA 704 and follow it west to the state park.

Maryland

Assateague Island National Seashore
Berlin, Maryland

This federally operated seashore is a great recreation getaway for beach lovers from all along the eastern seaboard. Here you can explore miles of beach, camp in a variety of settings, and engage in every manner of activity the waterfront offers, from surf fishing to beach driving, kayaking, kiteboarding, swimming, and crabbing. All the fun activities notwithstanding, Assateague

Figure 41. Kiteboarding on the landward side of Assateague Island National Seashore.

Island National Seashore is best known for its wild ponies. The ponies have resided on the island for upwards of three hundred years and never fail to excite first-time park visitors, who immediately rush for the camera to photograph the appealing animals.

The camping facilities cater to many different types of campers with two distinctive camping areas on the ocean side and on the bay side of the island. At the south end of the island, in Virginia, is part of Chincoteague National Wildlife Refuge; a visit to the refuge enhances a visit to the national seashore.

The Beach/Coast

Assateague Island is shared by Maryland and Virginia. The Maryland portion of the island makes up most of Assateague Island National Seashore, which features 19 miles of shoreline (with an additional two miles of shoreline in Assateague Island State Park). From the state line, the Virginia part of island is managed primarily by the U.S. Fish and Wildlife Service as Chincoteague National Wildlife Refuge. Beach usage is much more restricted at the refuge. This is no particular inconvenience with the adjoining national seashore is so large.

A beach with lifeguards lies just inside the national seashore entrance. This area is known as North Beach and is the only area of the national seashore with lifeguards. A bathhouse and picnic area are conveniently close. Crossovers lead over the dunes to the beach. Farther down the beach the dunes begin to rise higher. The Oceanside Campground lies on the landward side of the high dunes. More dune crossovers allow campers to access the beach easily. Next is the South Beach area, which also has restrooms and parking. Beyond this is the off-road-vehicle zone, where four-wheel-drive cars can get onto the beach. A convenient air pump allows visitors to add air back to their tires after lowering the pressure for beach driving. The beach continues for 12 miles to the Virginia border and the wildlife refuge. Emergency phones and backcountry campsites are the only amenities in the southern part of the national seashore.

The Campground

Campsites can be found here to suit every kind of camper except those who want water and electricity hookups. However, RV campers should not shy away from this destination despite the handicap. The campsites are pleasant and are conveniently located close to either the Atlantic or Sinepuxent Bay. The Oceanside Campground offers two loops with drive-up campsites. The road and pull-ins are paved. Vegetation is spare in the level sites. Then you reach the Oceanside walk-in campsites. These sites are spread over a large area. Leave your car at the parking area and walk a short distance to various sites. Some are set into thick brush, which offers shelter from the wind. Other sites are out in the open, which could be good for cooling and insect-ridding breezes. Many of the sites are on the sand and just a tall dune away from the Atlantic Ocean.

The Bayside Campground offers a different atmosphere in its three loops stretched out on a peninsula jutting into Sinepuxent Bay. It has more trees, though grassy areas are interspersed with those that have trees. Cedars provide coveted shade. The campsites are all drive-up and are large and well separated from one another. Some sites come with a watery view. Be apprised that the B Loop here is a "no generators" loop. First-time visitors may need to scout for the site that feels right; after coming here, you will have figured out the type of site you prefer. Reservations are recommended during the warm season, as the campground fills daily from June through August and on many weekends from May through October.

Human and Natural History

The old boathouse for the United States Lifesaving Service is located at the seashore and is now a museum. The men of this group, founded in 1871, were the precursors to what is now the U.S. Coast Guard. They were stationed along the country's ocean and Great Lakes shorelines, patrolling the waters for ships in trouble, steering them away from danger if possible. Assateague Island had four lifesaving stations. When a ship ran aground the men would rush to the scene and fire a rope from the shore to allow people to escape from the ship before it broke apart. If the ship was too far away from shore for this, the lifesavers would row through the rough waters to rescue sailors. The Lifesaving Service was in business for forty-four years, saving those in distress all over the nation. While you are here, take time to see the Boathouse Museum and remember these heroes of the past.

What to Do

Assateague Island is a great place for active beachgoers. Out here you see many visitors lounging at the beach but also others surf fishing, beachcombing, surfing, or heading into the off-road-vehicle area and the less heavily visited part of the beach. You don't need a license to surf fish in the national seashore. The park has three excellent trails for learning about the island ecosystem. Hike the Life of the Marsh Trail, the Life of the Forest Trail, and the Life of the Dunes Trail for your ecology overview. Over on Sinepuxent Bay, kiteboarders run the waters. If you don't have your own gear, rent a canoe to paddle the bay or a clam rig to go clamming. The rental center near the Bayside Picnic Area also rents bikes. The island is great for pedaling—flat roads make cycling a pleasure for everyone. You can even bike all the way to the national park visitor center on the mainland via the pedestrian bridge over Sinepuxent Bay. Of course, seeing the famous Assateague Island ponies is always popular, too.

What's Nearby

The south end of the island is where Chincoteague National Wildlife Refuge lies. It has a beach area, Toms Cove Beach, which has a bathhouse. The refuge has more trails to explore and roads to bike as well as the Assateague Lighthouse. The beacon can be reached by a quarter-mile trail off the Wildlife Loop. The three-mile Wildlife Loop is closed to cars before 3:00 p.m. The Swan Cove Trail takes you to the beach. The Woodland Trail goes to an overlook where wild ponies roam. The refuge is also a birding destination on the Eastern Flyway. The drive to the refuge and Toms Cove takes about 75 minutes; they can only be reached by returning to the mainland.

Information

Assateague Island National Seashore
7206 Seashore Lane
Berlin, MD 21811
(410) 641-1441, www.nps.gov/asis; reservations (800) 365-CAMP, www.reservations.nps.gov
Open: Year-round
Sites: 41 Oceanside drive-up sites, 62 Oceanside walk-in sites, 49 Bayside drive-up sites
Amenities: Oceanside sites have picnic table, upright grill; bayside sites have picnic table, fire ring
Registration: By phone, Internet, or at campground ranger station booth
Facilities: Cold showers, vault toilets, water spigots

Fees: $20 per night

Directions: From US 113 in Berlin, Maryland, take MD 376 east for 4 miles to MD 611. Turn right on MD 611 and follow it for 4.5 miles to Bayberry Drive, on Assateague Island. Turn right on Bayberry Drive and follow it 2 miles into the national seashore and the park campgrounds.

Assateague Island State Park

Berlin, Maryland

If you like a lot of sandy open beach and you like beach camping, come to Assateague Island State Park. This is what is known as a camping park. The campground is a primary draw, along with the beach, of course. Despite heavy visitation, the campground, beach, and park facilities are well cared for and in great shape. Maryland takes pride in its most popular state park. To demonstrate commitment to this area, the state spent $11 million restoring the dunes here, which back against the Atlantic Ocean. This two-mile-wide park is sandwiched between sections of the much larger Assateague Island National Seashore, which runs for miles on either side of the state park, effectively enhancing the size of this destination. The camping area covers a large portion of the state park property, with its 350 campsites just behind the restored dunes, and makes for a great base to explore this barrier island getaway that is the most northerly in this book.

The Beach/Coast

On your approach to Assateague Island you leave the mainland and take a bridge over Sinepuxent Bay, which is an arm of Chincoteague Bay, the es-

Figure 42. The famed ponies of Assateague Island State Park.

tuarine waters that divide Assateague Island from the mainland. Once on Assateague Island, you soon enter the state park, reaching park facilities that make it easy for ocean lovers to enjoy the coastline. The main beachside bathhouse is much more than just a bathhouse. It has outdoor showers, indoor showers, a camp store, and a snack bar.

A boardwalk leads over the dunes from the bathhouse to reach the beach. Here visitors can enjoy two miles of state park beach along the Atlantic Ocean. The beach is light tan sand and is wide enough to accommodate many people. Lifeguards are stationed here during the summer swimming season. As one moves down the beach toward the campground, the dunes are protected by fences to keep people and the famous wild ponies of Assateague Island from trampling the dune vegetation. Twelve dune crossovers at the campground channel visitors between campsites and the beach that everyone has come to enjoy. There are miles more of seashore to visit just south of the state park, in the national seashore part of the island.

The Campground

As already mentioned, this is a camping park; it has a lot of campsites—350 all told. They are strung out parallel to the Atlantic Ocean in a series of ten loops separated from the beach by dunes. The campground itself is mostly level but has some dunes in the midst of its loops. There is minimal vegetation of any kind; only some wind-pruned small trees and brush. This is a sandy place. The campground roads and campsite pull-ins are paved, minimizing problems of cars and RVs getting stuck in the sand.

Loops A–G are similar to one another. Each has 30 campsites, beach access, and a bathhouse either in the loop or very nearby. Tent campers pitch shelters on the sand beside the auto pull-ins. The sites are average to small. A screen shelter is a big help here for protection from the bugs and to provide shade. RV campers take note of Loop H. It has the 39 sites with electricity, which could air-condition your rig—the only such sites in the campground. However, even there you will be dry camping because Loop H, like all the others, has community water spigots rather than water hookups. Loop I is the largest of them all, with 110 campsites and two bathhouses. Loop J is at the end of the campground. The sites closest to the beach go first, but all sites are quite close to the beach.

This state park is popular, filling daily from mid-June through August and on September weekends. Reservations are highly recommended. One of the big attractions of the state park is the fact that it has hot showers, as opposed to the campground at nearby Assateague Island National Seashore.

Human and Natural History

Assateague Island is known for its wild ponies. But unlike those of Ocracoke Island in North Carolina's Outer Banks, which are believed to derive from shipwrecked Spanish horses, the Assateague ponies are descendants of domesticated ponies that likely arrived when mainland farmers brought them to the island to avoid the taxing of livestock. These horses are smaller than average. Life on the island is harsh. The ponies' poor diet of salt marsh cordgrass and other salty vegetation causes them to drink twice as much water as other horses, resulting in a stocky, bloated appearance.

Despite urgings from state and national park officials not to do so, visitors continue to feed the ponies. When this happens they can become a nuisance in the campground, foraging through trash, nosing into coolers, and leaving a mess. This also increases the odds of their getting hit by cars. Humans can get hurt, too: every year, people get bitten or kicked by the ponies. The state park is strict about not feeding the ponies and won't hesitate to fine offenders. So keep the ponies as wild as possible by not feeding them.

What to Do

Warnings aside, the ponies bring in visitors to the park. Everybody wants a picture of the ponies. But the beach is an even bigger draw. It is less crowded out here on Assateague Island than on the beaches of nearby Ocean City. Some visitors use the park as a base to visit Ocean City, returning in the evenings. The Nature Center is conveniently located between the D and E loops in the campground. Interpretive programs are held daily. Canoeing the bay side of the island is popular on calm days.

Bicycling is big on Assateague. You can pedal the state park and national seashore roads, which are very level. If you want to make a climb and enjoy a view, pedal over Sinepuxent Bay on the bridge for pedestrians and cyclists that runs alongside the main bridge over the bay.

But most of all, this is a camping park, so don't be surprised if your camping neighbor makes a daily commute only between the campsite and the beach, using the rest of the time strictly for relaxation—just camping.

What's Nearby

Of course, being bordered by the large Assateague Island National Seashore makes it easy to explore Assateague Island beyond the state park boundaries. The national seashore has more beaches to explore, hiking trails, canoe and bicycle rentals, and beach driving access with a permit. The tourist town of Ocean City lures in people who like to camp on Assateague but also enjoy urban amenities. Ocean City has everything you would expect from a busy beachside getaway, including lots of other people. It's fun to hit the boardwalk and see who else is enjoying the Maryland seashore.

Information

Assateague Island State Park
7307 Stephen Decatur Highway
Berlin, MD 21811
(410) 641-2120, www.dnr.state.md.us/publiclands; reservations (888) 432-CAMP
Open: May through October
Sites: 39 electric, 311 other
Amenities: Picnic table, fire ring; some sites have electricity
Registration: By phone or at campground office
Facilities: Hot showers, flush toilets, camp store, pay phone
Fees: Sites with electricity $40 per night; other sites $30 per night
Directions: From US 113 in Berlin, Maryland, take MD 376 east for 4 miles to MD 611. Turn right on MD 611 and follow it for 4.5 miles to the state park, which is dead ahead after you reach Assateague Island.

Johnny Molloy is an outdoor writer based in Johnson City, Tennessee. A native Tennessean, he was born in Memphis and moved to Knoxville in 1980 to attend the University of Tennessee. It was in Knoxville that he developed his love of the natural world, which has since become the primary focus of his life.

It all started on a backpacking foray into the Great Smoky Mountains National Park. That first trip, though a disaster, unleashed an innate love of the outdoors that has led to his spending over a hundred nights in the wild per year over the past twenty-five years, backpacking and canoe camping throughout our country.

After graduating from the University of Tennessee with a degree in economics, he continued to spend an ever increasing amount of time in natural places, becoming more skilled in a variety of environments. Friends enjoyed his adventure stories; one suggested he write a book. He pursued his friend's idea, and soon he had parlayed his love of the outdoors into an occupation.

The results of his efforts are more than twenty-seven books, including hiking, camping, and paddling guidebooks, comprehensive guides to particular areas, and true outdoor adventure books. Molloy has also written numerous magazine articles and for Web sites. He continues to write and travel extensively to all corners of the United States, undertaking a variety of outdoor pursuits. For the latest on Johnny, please visit www.johnnymolloy.com.